Cooking Light®

BIG BOOK OF

SALADS

ISBN-13: 978-0-8487-3646-0
ISBN-10: 0-8487-3646-X
Library of Congress Control Number: 2011943932
Printed in the United States of America
First Printing 2012

Be sure to check with your health-care provider before making any changes in your diet.

Oxmoor House
VP, Publishing Director: Jim Childs
Creative Director: Felicity Keane
Brand Manager: Michelle Turner Aycock
Senior Editor: Heather Averett
Managing Editor: Rebecca Benton

Cooking Light® BIG BOOK OF SALADS
Editor: Shaun Chavis
Project Editor: Diane Rose
Senior Designer: J. Shay McNamee
Director, Test Kitchen: Elizabeth Tyler Austin
Assistant Directors, Test Kitchen: Julie Christopher, Julie Gunter
Test Kitchen Professionals: Wendy Ball, RD; Allison E. Cox; Victoria E. Cox; Margaret Monroe Dickey; Alyson Moreland Haynes; Stefanie Maloney; Callie Nash; Catherine Crowell Steele; Leah Van Deren
Photography Director: Jim Bathie
Senior Photo Stylist: Kay E. Clarke
Associate Photo Stylist: Katherine Eckert Coyne
Assistant Photo Stylist: Mary Louise Menendez
Senior Production Manager: Greg A. Amason

Contributors
Compositor: Teresa Cole
Copy Editors: Jacqueline Giovanelli, Tara Trenary
Proofreaders: Julie Hall Bosché, Dolores Hydock
Indexer: Nanette Cardon
Interns: Erin Bishop; Maribeth Browning; Jessica Cox, RD; Laura Hoxworth; Alison Loughman; Lindsay A. Rozier
Test Kitchen Professionals: Erica Hopper, Kathleen Royal Phillips
Photographers: Beau Gustafson, Lee Harrelson, Mary Britton Senseney
Photo Stylists: Anna Pollock, Leslie Simpson, Caitlin Von Horn

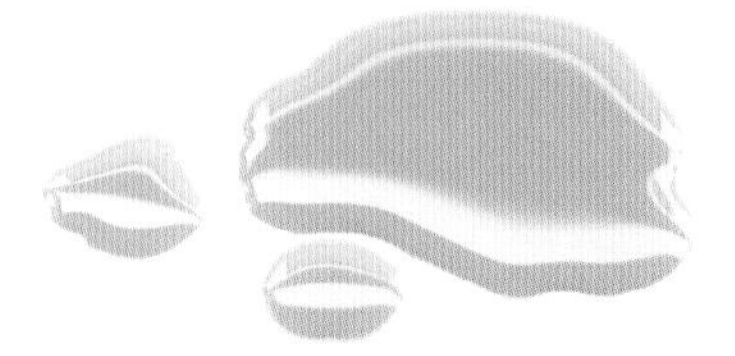

Time Home Entertainment Inc.
Publisher: Richard Fraiman
VP, Strategy & Business Development: Steven Sandonato
Executive Director, Marketing Services: Carol Pittard
Executive Director, Retail & Special Sales: Tom Mifsud
Executive Director, New Product Development: Peter Harper
Director, Bookazine Development & Marketing: Laura Adam
Publishing Director: Joy Butts
Finance Director: Glenn Buonocore
Associate General Counsel: Helen Wan

Cooking Light®
Editor: Scott Mowbray
Creative Director: Carla Frank
Deputy Editor: Phillip Rhodes
Executive Editor, Food: Ann Taylor Pittman
Special Publications Editor: Mary Simpson Creel, MS, RD
Senior Food Editor: Julianna Grimes
Senior Editor: Cindy Hatcher
Associate Food Editor: Timothy Q. Cebula
Assistant Editor, Nutrition: Sidney Fry, MS, RD
Assistant Editors: Kimberly Holland, Phoebe Wu
Test Kitchen Director: Vanessa T. Pruett
Assistant Test Kitchen Director: Tiffany Vickers Davis
Recipe Testers and Developers: Robin Bashinsky, Adam Hickman, Deb Wise
Art Directors: Fernande Bondarenko, Shawna Kalish
Associate Art Director: Rachel Cardina Lasserre
Junior Designer: Hagen Stegall
Photo Director: Kristen Schaefer
Assistant Photo Editor: Amy Delaune
Senior Photographer: Randy Mayor
Senior Photo Stylist: Cindy Barr
Photo Stylist: Leigh Ann Ross
Chief Food Stylist: Charlotte Autry
Senior Food Stylist: Kellie Gerber Kelley
Food Styling Assistant: Blakeslee Wright
Copy Chief: Maria Parker Hopkins
Assistant Copy Chief: Susan Roberts
Research Editor: Michelle Gibson Daniels
Editorial Production Director: Liz Rhoades
Production Editor: Hazel R. Eddins
Assistant Production Editor: Josh Rutledge
Administrative Coordinator: Carol D. Johnson
Cookinglight.com Editor: Allison Long Lowery
Nutrition Editor: Holley Johnson Grainger, MS, RD
Production Assistant: Mallory Daugherty

To order additional publications, call 1-800-765-6400 or 1-800-491-0551.

For more books to enrich your life, visit **oxmoorhouse.com**

To search, savor, and share thousands of recipes, visit **myrecipes.com**

Cover: *Farro Salad with Roasted Beets, Watercress, and Poppy Seed Dressing, page 152*

Cooking Light

BIG BOOK OF SALADS

Oxmoor House®

ROAST CHICKEN SALAD WITH PEACHES, GOAT CHEESE, AND PECANS, p. 193

CONTENTS

CREAMY
BUTTERMILK-HERB
POTATO SALAD, p. 51

WELCOME

THE SALAD RENAISSANCE IS HERE! WITH NEW FARMERS' MARKETS OPENING ALL over the country, regionally sourced fruits and vegetables filling grocery produce sections, and international ingredients showing up on supermarket shelves, there are more fresh, flavorful choices than ever before. Salads are the ultimate celebration of what you're now able to bring to your table: On just one plate, you can combine the season's best, juiciest offerings, showcasing their vibrant color, wonderful aromas, and mouthwatering deliciousness.

So enjoy—even have fun—with the vegetables, fruits, and herbs that lure you from their market stands. Experiment with cutting food into different shapes—the **Shaved Summer Squash Salad with Prosciutto Crisps** (page 87) turns zucchini and yellow squash into lovely ribbons. Pull the leaves off Brussels sprouts to create petal-shaped mini-bowls for bacon, maple syrup, and pecans in the **Brussels Sprouts Salad with Warm Bacon Vinaigrette** (page 45). Add edible flowers to beautifully complement the colors in **Beets with Walnuts, Goat Cheese, and Baby Greens** (page 37).

Cooking Light Big Book of Salads is a treasure trove of helpful information and yummy recipes. In this cookbook you'll find:

- TIP BOXES throughout to show you how to spot and care for the best in-season produce, and special features that show you **how to baby your greens** (page 38), **how to buy good and sustainable seafood** (page 232), and **how to select the right pastas and grains for a salad** (pages 108 and 144).
- DRESSINGS, VINAIGRETTES, AND TOPPINGS that give you plenty of options to inspire your own salad creations. Try the **Herbed Lemon-Buttermilk Dressing** (page 22); it's our version of ranch dressing. Get ideas for tasty topping combos from the **100-Calorie Salad Boosters** sprinkled throughout the book.
- RECIPES FOR LIGHTENED FAVORITES like **Grilled Chicken Caesar Salad** (page 189), **Southwestern Cobb Salad** (page 195), **Creamy Chicken Salad** (page 187), and **Southwestern-Style Shrimp Taco Salad** made with spicy shrimp and served in a crunchy shell (page 264).
- PLENTY OF COOKOUT CLASSICS for a crowd, such as **Creamy Buttermilk-Herb Potato Salad** (page 51), **Panzanella** (page 135), or **Jalapeño-Lime Slaw** (page 66).
- SALADS THAT FIT YOUR LIFESTYLE: **Superfast** recipes are ready to eat in 20 minutes or less. We've also flagged **Kid-Friendly, Make-Ahead, Portable,** and **Vegetarian** recipes so that it's easy to pick something for a weeknight dinner for the family or for lunch to take to work.
- NUTRITION INFORMATION for every recipe.

Cooking Light Big Book of Salads, created by our dedicated staff of culinary professionals and registered dietitians, gives you all the secrets to seriously tasty salads. Dig in!

The *Cooking Light* Editors

vinaigrettes, dressings & toppings

Homemade dressing is a treat: It can make even a simple plate of greens memorable. Here are 22 easy ways to add great flavor to nature's best bounty.

FOUR-HERB GREEN GODDESS DRESSING, p. 11 →

KID-FRIENDLY / MAKE-AHEAD / PORTABLE / SUPERFAST / VEGETARIAN

CLASSIC VINAIGRETTE

This classic vinaigrette recipe is so simple you'll soon know it by heart. It's great on steamed fresh veggies and salads, or drizzled on sprouts in a sandwich. Experiment with different vinegars to change things up from time to time.

1½ tablespoons red wine vinegar
1 tablespoon chopped shallots
1 tablespoon Dijon mustard
¼ teaspoon salt
⅛ teaspoon freshly ground black pepper
3 tablespoons extra-virgin olive oil

1. Combine vinegar, shallots, mustard, salt, and pepper. Gradually add oil, stirring until incorporated. Store in an airtight container in refrigerator up to 1 week. Yield: 6 tablespoons (serving size: 1½ tablespoons).

CALORIES 94; **FAT** 10.1g (sat 1.4g, mono 7.4g, poly 1.1g); **PROTEIN** 0.1g; **CARB** 0.7g; **FIBER** 0g; **CHOL** 0mg; **IRON** 0.1mg; **SODIUM** 178mg; **CALC** 2mg

SHALLOTS

Shallots are the secret ingredient that adds a mild onion flavor to dressings and sauces. Choose shallots that are firm to the touch, and store them for up to a week at room temperature.

KID-FRIENDLY / MAKE-AHEAD
PORTABLE / SUPERFAST

FOUR-HERB GREEN GODDESS DRESSING

Drape over greens, or serve as a dip for your favorite summery crudités.

1 cup plain fat-free Greek yogurt
½ cup reduced-fat mayonnaise
2 teaspoons Worcestershire sauce
2 teaspoons fresh lemon juice
½ teaspoon hot pepper sauce
3 canned anchovy fillets
1 garlic clove, minced
⅔ cup fresh parsley leaves
¼ cup fresh tarragon leaves
¼ cup chopped fresh chives
¼ cup fresh chervil leaves

1. Place first 7 ingredients in a blender or food processor; process until smooth. Add parsley and remaining ingredients; process until herbs are minced. Store in an airtight container in refrigerator up to 2 days. Yield: 1½ cups (serving size: about 2½ tablespoons).

CALORIES 36; **FAT** 1.8g (sat 0g, mono 0.1g, poly 0.8g); **PROTEIN** 2.6g; **CARB** 3.6g; **FIBER** 0.1g; **CHOL** 1mg; **IRON** 0.4mg; **SODIUM** 171mg; **CALC** 30mg

HOW TO

MAKE HOMEMADE VINAIGRETTE

A GOOD VINAIGRETTE is a thing of beauty. Grab a bowl, whisk together oil and vinegar, add a pinch of salt, and plain lettuce springs to life, veggies go from bland to bold, and meat finds a tangy marinade.

Vinaigrette may be easy to prepare, but there is a method to its magic. The keys to success start with good ingredients and end with emulsification, thoroughly blending the oil's fat molecules and the watery vinegar. Adding a touch of Dijon mustard helps the vinaigrette emulsify. From there, flavor as you like. Try a bit of honey, fresh herbs, toasted spices, or minced shallots. You can also change the types of oils and acids: Try lemon or lime juice in place of the vinegar, or experiment with different flavored vinegars. A nut oil in place of olive oil gives vinaigrettes a decadent taste (for suggestions, see "Beyond Olive Oil" on page 28). To make a successful vinaigrette, follow the steps at right.

STEP 1

Build a Flavor Base

Finely mince 2 tablespoons shallots so pieces will incorporate easily and spread throughout your dressing. Place in a bowl with 1 teaspoon Dijon mustard.

STEP 2

Add an Acid

Pour 2 tablespoons sherry vinegar into the mixture with ¼ teaspoon kosher salt and ¼ teaspoon freshly ground black pepper; whisk to combine.

STEP 3

Whisk in Oil

Slowly pour 6 tablespoons extra-virgin olive oil into the mixture, whisking to create a creamy, emulsified finish.

Success!

When properly emulsified, ingredients are suspended throughout the mix, as on the right.

KID-FRIENDLY / MAKE-AHEAD / PORTABLE SUPERFAST / VEGETARIAN

EASY HERB VINAIGRETTE

This dressing lasts only a couple of days because of the fresh herbs.

9 tablespoons white wine vinegar
1½ tablespoons honey
½ teaspoon salt
1 cup canola oil
3 tablespoons chopped fresh basil
3 tablespoons minced fresh chives

1. Combine first 3 ingredients in a medium bowl; slowly add oil, stirring with a whisk until combined. Stir in basil and chives. Store in an airtight container in refrigerator up to 2 days. Yield: 1 cup (serving size: 1 tablespoon).

CALORIES 160; **FAT** 17.2g (sat 1.2g, mono 10.2g, poly 5.1g); **PROTEIN** 0.1g; **CARB** 2.1g; **FIBER** 0.1g; **CHOL** 0mg; **IRON** 0mg; **SODIUM** 89mg; **CALC** 2mg

MAKE-AHEAD / PORTABLE / SUPERFAST

CHILE-GARLIC VINAIGRETTE

Use this piquant dressing on green salads loaded with shredded raw vegetables like zucchini, yellow squash, daikon radish, and cucumber.

1 tablespoon chopped serrano chile
1/2 teaspoon salt
6 garlic cloves, crushed
1 canned anchovy fillet
3 tablespoons red wine vinegar
2 tablespoons water
2 tablespoons fresh lemon juice
1 1/2 tablespoons extra-virgin olive oil

1. Combine first 4 ingredients in a mortar; mash to a paste with a pestle. Combine chile paste mixture, vinegar, and remaining ingredients in a small bowl, stirring with a whisk. Store in an airtight container in refrigerator up to 1 week. Yield: 3/4 cup (serving size: 1 tablespoon).

CALORIES 21; **FAT** 1.7g (sat 0.2g, mono 1.2g, poly 0.2g); **PROTEIN** 0.3g; **CARB** 1.1g; **FIBER** 0.1g; **CHOL** 1mg; **IRON** 0.7mg; **SODIUM** 266mg; **CALC** 8mg

KID-FRIENDLY / MAKE-AHEAD / PORTABLE SUPERFAST / VEGETARIAN

CRANBERRY VINAIGRETTE

Serve with arugula and goat cheese for a tart, peppery salad. This thick dressing is also delicious spread on turkey sandwiches, or with roasted meats such as chicken, pork, and duck.

1 cup cranberry juice
½ cup chopped fresh or frozen cranberries, thawed
1 tablespoon extra-virgin olive oil
1 tablespoon red wine vinegar
1 tablespoon honey
2 teaspoons minced fresh chives
⅛ teaspoon salt
⅛ teaspoon freshly ground black pepper

1. Place juice and cranberries in a small saucepan; bring to a boil. Cook until reduced to ¼ cup (about 5 minutes). Combine cranberry mixture, oil, and remaining ingredients in a small bowl; stir well with a whisk. Store in an airtight container in refrigerator up to 1 week. Yield: ½ cup (serving size: 4 teaspoons).

CALORIES 53; **FAT** 2.3g (sat 0.3g, mono 1.6g, poly 0.2g); **PROTEIN** 0.1g; **CARB** 8.4g; **FIBER** 0.5g; **CHOL** 0mg; **IRON** 0.1mg; **SODIUM** 52mg; **CALC** 8mg

KID-FRIENDLY / MAKE-AHEAD / SUPERFAST

CREAMY CAESAR DRESSING

Lighten up a traditional Caesar salad dressing by replacing some of the oil with fat-free yogurt. The Dijon mustard, red wine vinegar, anchovy paste, and Worcestershire sauce guarantee plenty of flavor.

1/3 cup plain fat-free yogurt
2 tablespoons fresh lemon juice
1 tablespoon olive oil
2 teaspoons red wine vinegar
2 teaspoons Worcestershire sauce
1 teaspoon anchovy paste
1 teaspoon Dijon mustard
1/2 teaspoon freshly ground black pepper
1 garlic clove, minced

1. Combine all ingredients in a bowl; stir well with a whisk. Store in an airtight container in refrigerator up to 2 days. Yield: ½ cup (serving size: 1 tablespoon).

CALORIES 26; **FAT** 1.8g (sat 0.2g, mono 1.3g, poly 0.2g); **PROTEIN** 0.8g; **CARB** 1.6g; **FIBER** 0g; **CHOL** 0mg; **IRON** 0.1mg; **SODIUM** 124mg; **CALC** 22mg

KID-FRIENDLY / MAKE-AHEAD / PORTABLE / SUPERFAST / VEGETARIAN

CREAMY RASPBERRY DRESSING ➤

You can have a bright spark of summer any time of year with this easy dressing. Make and refrigerate it up to a week in advance. It's delicious on a spinach salad with some chopped hard-cooked egg and shredded carrot, or on a fruit salad with plenty of hulled strawberries and sliced peaches.

1/3 cup honey
1/4 cup raspberry vinegar
1/4 cup plain fat-free yogurt
1 tablespoon Dijon mustard
2 teaspoons olive oil
1/4 teaspoon salt
1/4 teaspoon freshly ground black pepper

1. Combine all ingredients; stir with a whisk until creamy. Store in an airtight container in refrigerator up to 1 week. Yield: ¾ cup (serving size: 3 tablespoons).

CALORIES 120; **FAT** 2.6g (sat 0.3g, mono 1.8g, poly 0.3g); **PROTEIN** 1.2g; **CARB** 25.1g; **FIBER** 0.1g; **CHOL** 0mg; **IRON** 0.4mg; **SODIUM** 257mg; **CALC** 39mg

MAKE-AHEAD / PORTABLE
SUPERFAST / VEGETARIAN

BLUE CHEESE DRESSING

Blue cheese can be made from cow's, goat's, or sheep's milk. What they have in common is that they are made with molds that create blue-green streaks and a distinctive flavor that gets stronger with age. For this dressing, use a younger blue cheese for a mild dressing, or use an older cheese for a bolder, more pungent dressing.

½ cup (2 ounces) crumbled blue cheese
½ cup plain fat-free yogurt
2 tablespoons light mayonnaise

1. Combine all ingredients in a small bowl. Cover and chill. Store in an airtight container in refrigerator up to 1 week. Yield: ¾ cup (serving size: 1 tablespoon).

CALORIES: 29; **FAT** 2g (sat 1g, mono 0.6g, poly 0.4g); **PROTEIN** 1.6g; **CARB** 1g; **FIBER** 0g; **CHOL** 5mg; **IRON** 0mg; **SODIUM** 92mg; **CALCIUM** 44mg

KID-FRIENDLY / MAKE-AHEAD / PORTABLE / SUPERFAST / VEGETARIAN

▲ ASIAN GINGER-CARROT DRESSING

Here's a healthier take on the flavorful dressing found on salads in Japanese restaurants across North America.

3 tablespoons finely shredded carrot
3 tablespoons mirin (sweet rice wine)
¼ cup minced peeled fresh ginger
¼ cup lower-sodium soy sauce
2 tablespoons rice vinegar

1. Combine all ingredients in a medium bowl, stirring with a whisk. Store in an airtight container in refrigerator up to 3 days. Yield: about 1 cup (serving size: 2 tablespoons).

CALORIES 21; **FAT** 0g (sat 0g, mono 0g, poly 0g); **PROTEIN** 0.6g; **CARB** 3g; **FIBER** 0.1g; **CHOL** 0mg; **IRON** 0.1mg; **SODIUM** 197mg; **CALC** 3mg

HOW TO

DRESS A SALAD

PERFECTLY DRESSED GREENS

A SOGGY PILE OF wilted greens makes for a sorry salad indeed. Tender greens like Boston lettuce, mâche, and arugula are delicate little things that perish at the mere rumor of mistreatment (tearing or roughly handling lettuce bruises it), but even crisp, hearty lettuces like romaine need to be treated with care. To keep them at their best, you need to consider three factors: time, volume, and temperature.

Only dress your greens just before serving, particularly when using vinaigrette: Oil quickly permeates the waxy surface of leafy greens, turning them dark green and droopy. If you've washed your greens, use a salad spinner or blot them delicately with paper towels to dry them. Water clinging to leaves will repel oil-based vinaigrettes and thin out creamy dressings, leading to bland salad.

Put dry greens in a salad bowl. Add less dressing than you think you'll need (to avoid overdressing), and pour it down the sides of the bowl, not directly onto the greens—you'll dress them more evenly this way. Gently toss, adding dressing as needed, until the greens are lightly coated. If you do overdress them, a quick whirl in the salad spinner will shake off any excess.

Finally, follow the lead of professional chefs and serve your salad on chilled plates to help keep the greens crisp as you enjoy them.

KID-FRIENDLY / MAKE-AHEAD / PORTABLE / SUPERFAST / VEGETARIAN

ESSENTIAL LEMON VINAIGRETTE

There's just something about that mix of lemon juice and olive oil—so Mediterranean, so irresistible.

1 tablespoon grated lemon rind
1 tablespoon minced fresh dill or 1 teaspoon dried dill
3 tablespoons fresh lemon juice
¼ teaspoon salt
¼ teaspoon freshly ground black pepper
2 tablespoons olive oil

1. Combine lemon rind and next 4 ingredients (through pepper) in a medium bowl, stirring with a whisk. Slowly add olive oil in a thin stream, stirring constantly with a whisk until combined. Store in an airtight container in refrigerator up to 2 days. Yield: 4 servings (serving size: 1¾ tablespoons).

CALORIES 64; **FAT** 6.8g (sat 0.9g, mono 4.9g, poly 0.7g); **PROTEIN** 0.1g; **CARB** 1.3g; **FIBER** 0.2g; **CHOL** 0mg; **IRON** 0.1mg; **SODIUM** 148mg; **CALC** 4mg

DILL

Fresh dill gives lemony, herbal essence to dressings, sauces, and fish.

KID-FRIENDLY / MAKE-AHEAD / PORTABLE SUPERFAST / VEGETARIAN

CUMIN VINAIGRETTE

Get the best flavor by grinding your own cumin. Buy whole seeds and toast them in a dry skillet over medium heat until they become fragrant. Grind them with a mortar and pestle, or in a coffee grinder dedicated only for spices.

1 teaspoon Dijon mustard
½ cup extra-virgin olive oil
1 teaspoon fresh lemon juice
2 teaspoons sherry vinegar
1 teaspoon cumin seeds, ground
1 tablespoon finely chopped fresh mint
¼ teaspoon salt
¼ teaspoon freshly ground black pepper

1. Place Dijon mustard in a bowl, and whisk in olive oil, lemon juice, and sherry vinegar. Add cumin, mint, salt, and pepper, stirring with a whisk. Store in an airtight container in refrigerator up to 10 days. Yield: ¾ cup (serving size: 1 tablespoon).

CALORIES 82; **FAT** 9.4g (sat 1.3g, mono 6.7g, poly 1.3g); **PROTEIN** 0g; **CARB** 0.3g; **FIBER** 0g; **CHOL** 0mg; **IRON** 0.1mg; **SODIUM** 60mg; **CALC** 2mg

KID-FRIENDLY / MAKE-AHEAD / PORTABLE / SUPERFAST / VEGETARIAN

HERBED LEMON-BUTTERMILK DRESSING ➤

This all-purpose dressing is similar to ranch dressing. It's great as a marinade on chicken, dressing on salad, and dip with cut-up vegetables.

3/4 cup nonfat buttermilk
1/3 cup reduced-fat mayonnaise
1 tablespoon grated lemon rind
1 tablespoon finely chopped onion
1 teaspoon finely chopped fresh chives
1 teaspoon finely chopped fresh basil
1 teaspoon finely chopped fresh thyme
2 teaspoons fresh lemon juice
2 teaspoons Dijon mustard
1/2 teaspoon coarsely ground black pepper
1/4 teaspoon salt
1 garlic clove, minced

1. Combine all ingredients, stirring with a whisk until dressing is well blended. Store in an airtight container in refrigerator up to 5 days; stir well before using. Yield: 1¼ cups (serving size: 1 tablespoon).

CALORIES 12; **FAT** 0.3g (sat 0g, mono 0.1g, poly 0.2g); **PROTEIN** 0.4g; **CARB** 1.9g; **FIBER** 0.1g; **CHOL** 0mg; **IRON** 0mg; **SODIUM** 89mg; **CALC** 13mg

BUTTERMILK

Buttermilk is a nice way to lend the same kind of tang as sour cream without as much fat. Now made by adding bacteria to milk, originally it was the milk left after churning butter.

KID-FRIENDLY / MAKE-AHEAD / PORTABLE SUPERFAST / VEGETARIAN

GINGER-SESAME VINAIGRETTE ➤

Try tossing this vinaigrette with salad greens or rice noodles, or use it as a dipping sauce for pot stickers or spring rolls. Many supermarkets stock miso with the refrigerated foods; if yours doesn't, you'll need to visit an Asian market.

1/2 cup rice wine vinegar
1/4 cup water
1/4 cup yellow miso (soybean paste)
1/4 cup chopped green onions
2 tablespoons sugar
2 tablespoons minced peeled fresh ginger
2 tablespoons lower-sodium soy sauce
4 teaspoons canola oil
2 teaspoons dark sesame oil

1. Combine first 3 ingredients in a medium bowl, stirring with a whisk until smooth. Stir in green onions and remaining ingredients. Store in an airtight container in refrigerator up to 5 days; stir well before using. Yield: about 1⅓ cups (serving size: 1 tablespoon).

CALORIES: 23; **FAT** 1.5g (sat 0.1g, mono 0.7g, poly 0.6g); **PROTEIN** 0.5g; **CARB** 2.1g; **FIBER** 0.1g; **CHOL** 0mg; **IRON** 0mg; **SODIUM** 192mg; **CALC** 0mg

KID-FRIENDLY / MAKE-AHEAD / PORTABLE / SUPERFAST / VEGETARIAN

ORANGE-POPPY SEED DRESSING

½ cup fresh orange juice
¼ cup honey
¼ cup canola oil
2 tablespoons champagne vinegar
⅛ teaspoon salt
1 teaspoon poppy seeds

1. Place first 5 ingredients in a blender; process until blended. Add poppy seeds; pulse once. Store in an airtight container in refrigerator up to 1 week. Yield: 1 cup plus 2 tablespoons (serving size: 1 tablespoon).

CALORIES 17; **FAT** 1.2g (sat 0.1g, mono 0.7g, poly 0.4g); **PROTEIN** 0g; **CARB** 1.7g; **FIBER** 0g; **CHOL** 0mg; **IRON** 0mg; **SODIUM** 7mg; **CALC** 1mg

POPPY SEEDS

These small seeds add crunch and subtle nuttiness to dressings and salads. They can go rancid, so store them in an airtight container in the refrigerator or freezer.

KID-FRIENDLY / MAKE-AHEAD / PORTABLE
SUPERFAST / VEGETARIAN

MUSTARD SEED-CHIVE VINAIGRETTE

We like this vinaigrette drizzled over gourmet salad greens, but it would also pair well with salmon. Olive oil—and olives themselves—offer heart-healthy monounsaturated fat.

2 tablespoons sherry vinegar
1 tablespoon water
1 teaspoon country-style Dijon mustard
1 teaspoon honey
1 tablespoon extra-virgin olive oil
2 tablespoons chopped fresh chives
½ teaspoon kosher salt
½ teaspoon mustard seeds
½ teaspoon freshly ground black pepper

1. Combine vinegar, 1 tablespoon water, mustard, and honey in a small bowl; stir with a whisk. Slowly add oil, stirring constantly with a whisk until well blended. Add chives, kosher salt, mustard seeds, and freshly ground black pepper; stir well with whisk. Store in an airtight container in refrigerator up to 2 days. Yield: ⅓ cup (serving size: about 1 tablespoon).

CALORIES 32; **FAT** 2.8g (sat 0.4g, mono 2g, poly 0.3g); **PROTEIN** 0.2g; **CARB** 1.7g; **FIBER** 0.1g; **CHOL** 0mg; **IRON** 0.1mg; **SODIUM** 212mg; **CALC** 4mg

KID-FRIENDLY / MAKE-AHEAD / PORTABLE / SUPERFAST / VEGETARIAN

SHALLOT AND GRAPEFRUIT DRESSING

Drizzle this zesty, citrusy dressing over mixed gourmet greens topped with goat cheese and roasted corn. You can squeeze your own grapefruit juice or look for fresh grapefruit juice in the produce section of the grocery store.

1 teaspoon olive oil
½ cup chopped shallots
2 cups fresh grapefruit juice (about 3 grapefruits)
2 tablespoons chopped fresh cilantro
2 teaspoons sugar
¼ teaspoon freshly ground black pepper
2 tablespoons olive oil

1. Heat 1 teaspoon oil in a large nonstick skillet over medium heat. Add shallots; cook 5 minutes or until golden brown. Stir in juice. Bring to a boil over medium-high heat, and cook until reduced to 1 cup (about 6 minutes). Remove from heat; cool.

2. Place grapefruit juice mixture, cilantro, sugar, and pepper in a blender; process until smooth. With blender on, slowly add 2 tablespoons oil; process until smooth. Store in an airtight container in refrigerator up to 2 days. Yield: 1 cup (serving size: 1 tablespoon).

CALORIES 35; **FAT** 2g (sat 0.3g, mono 1.5g, poly 0.2g); **PROTEIN** 0.3g; **CARB** 4.2g; **FIBER** 0.1g; **CHOL** 0mg; **IRON** 0.1mg; **SODIUM** 1mg; **CALC** 4mg

KID-FRIENDLY / MAKE-AHEAD / PORTABLE / SUPERFAST / VEGETARIAN

ORANGE-SESAME SALAD DRESSING

½ cup fresh orange juice (about 2 large oranges)
⅓ cup rice wine vinegar
2 tablespoons sesame seeds
1 tablespoon Chinese hot mustard
1 teaspoon sugar
¼ teaspoon kosher salt
1 garlic clove, minced
2 tablespoons canola oil
1 teaspoon dark sesame oil

1. Combine first 7 ingredients in a medium bowl. Slowly drizzle oils into juice mixture, stirring constantly with a whisk. Store in an airtight container in refrigerator up to 1 week. Yield: 1½ cups (serving size: 4 teaspoons).

CALORIES 27; **FAT** 2.3g (sat 0.2g, mono 1.2g, poly 0.8g); **PROTEIN** 0.2g; **CARB** 1.2g; **FIBER** 0.1g; **CHOL** 0mg; **IRON** 0.2mg; **SODIUM** 45mg; **CALC** 11mg

BEYOND OLIVE OIL

Gourmet oils give everyday fare new complexity and verve. If you're well-acquainted with the bottle of extra-virgin olive oil in your pantry, then it's time to get to know specialty oils.

WALNUT Like hazelnut, walnut oil is a great flavorful addition to most vinaigrettes. It has a light golden color, just slightly darker than vegetable oil, and a full-bodied nutty aroma.

ROASTED PEANUT Look for "toasted" peanut oil on the label. It will be darker than plain peanut oil with a surprisingly strong flavor, like fresh-packed peanuts.

HAZELNUT With a toasty, smooth, delicate, buttery flavor, hazelnut oil is an excellent substitute for vegetable oils in most vinaigrettes. It also has a golden hue.

PISTACHIO Slightly thicker than other nut oils, pistachio oil has a faintly sweet flavor with a lingering finish. The darker pistachio oil is, the more flavor it has.

AVOCADO The oil is extracted from the flesh (not the seed) of ripe fruits. The oil can range in color from pale to dark green. Dark avocado oil has a slightly nutty, full-bodied taste.

TRUFFLE A truffle is a highly prized mushroom that grows underground. Truffle oil is usually olive or grapeseed oil infused with the mushroom. It has an intense, earthy flavor with a pungent aroma.

KID-FRIENDLY / MAKE-AHEAD / PORTABLE SUPERFAST / VEGETARIAN

WALNUT OIL VINAIGRETTE

You can easily use another specialty oil in place of the walnut oil here—hazelnut or pistachio would be delicious.

¼ cup red wine vinegar
2 tablespoons minced shallots
2 tablespoons walnut oil
2 tablespoons honey
1 tablespoon fresh lemon juice
½ teaspoon salt
¼ teaspoon freshly ground black pepper

1. Combine all ingredients, stirring with a whisk. Store in an airtight container in refrigerator up to 1 week. Yield: ⅔ cup (serving size: about 1 tablespoon).

CALORIES 39; **FAT** 2.7g (sat 0.3g, mono 0.6g, poly 1.7g); **PROTEIN** 0.1g; **CARB** 4g; **FIBER** 0g; **CHOL** 0mg; **IRON** 0.1mg; **SODIUM** 118mg; **CALC** 1mg

KID-FRIENDLY / MAKE-AHEAD
PORTABLE / VEGETARIAN

SWEET CHIPOTLE SNACK MIX

¼ cup sugar
1 teaspoon salt
1 teaspoon ground chipotle chile pepper
½ teaspoon ground cumin
½ teaspoon dried oregano
½ teaspoon chili powder
1 large egg white
1 cup slivered almonds
1 cup unsalted cashews
1 cup unsalted pumpkinseed kernels

1. Preheat oven to 325°.
2. Combine first 6 ingredients in a small bowl; stir with a whisk.
3. Place egg white in a large bowl; stir with a whisk until foamy. Add almonds, cashews, and pumpkinseeds; toss well to coat. Sprinkle with spice mixture; toss well to coat. Spread mixture in an even layer on a baking sheet lined with parchment paper. Bake at 325° for 15 minutes, stirring once. Turn oven off. Remove pan from oven; stir snack mix. Immediately return pan to oven for an additional 15 minutes (leave oven off). Remove pan from oven, and place on a wire rack; cool completely. Store snack mix in an airtight container at room temperature up to 2 weeks. Yield: about 3½ cups (serving size: 3 tablespoons).

CALORIES 130; **FAT** 9.7g (sat 1.4g, mono 5.8g, poly 2g); **PROTEIN** 4.5g; **CARB** 7.3g; **FIBER** 1.1g; **CHOL** 0mg; **IRON** 1.1mg; **SODIUM** 175mg; **CALC** 23mg

KID-FRIENDLY / MAKE-AHEAD / PORTABLE / SUPERFAST / VEGETARIAN

CRISP CROUTONS

6 cups (½-inch) cubes sourdough or French bread (6 ounces)
1 tablespoon butter, melted
1 teaspoon paprika
1 teaspoon onion powder

1. Preheat oven to 350°.
2. Combine all ingredients in a roasting or jelly-roll pan; toss well to coat. Bake at 350° for 20 minutes or until toasted, turning once. Store in an airtight container at room temperature up to 2 days. Yield: 6 cups (serving size: 2 tablespoons).

CALORIES 24; **FAT** 0.7g (sat 0.4g, mono 0.2g, poly 0.1g); **PROTEIN** 0.7g; **CARB** 4g; **FIBER** 0.2g; **CHOL** 1mg; **IRON** 0.2mg; **SODIUM** 48mg; **CALC** 6mg

100-CALORIE SALAD BOOSTERS

Start with 1½ cups of fresh mixed greens. Add a tablespoon of your favorite vinaigrette. Then pile on the good stuff. There are some combinations that are no-brainers—this family of flavors is one of them.

¼ CUP FRESH PEAR SLICES

+

1 TABLESPOON CHOPPED TOASTED WALNUTS

+

½ OUNCE GOAT CHEESE

KID-FRIENDLY / MAKE-AHEAD / PORTABLE / SUPERFAST / VEGETARIAN

SWEET SPICED ALMONDS

1 cup sliced almonds
1/3 cup packed brown sugar
1 teaspoon ground cinnamon
1/2 teaspoon ground coriander
1/2 teaspoon ground cumin
1 large egg white, lightly beaten
Cooking spray

1. Preheat oven to 325°.
2. Combine almonds and next 4 ingredients (through cumin) in a small bowl. Stir in egg white. Spread mixture evenly onto a foil-lined baking sheet coated with cooking spray. Bake at 325° for 10 minutes. Stir mixture; bake an additional 15 minutes or until crisp. Transfer foil to a wire rack; cool almond mixture. Break almond mixture into small pieces. Store in an airtight container at room temperature up to 1 week. Yield: 2 cups (serving size: 1 tablespoon).

CALORIES 27; **FAT** 1.5g (sat 0.1g, mono 1g, poly 0.4g); **PROTEIN** 0.8g; **CARB** 2.9g; **FIBER** 0.4g; **CHOL** 0mg; **IRON** 0.2mg; **SODIUM** 3mg; **CALC** 11mg

KID-FRIENDLY / MAKE-AHEAD / PORTABLE SUPERFAST / VEGETARIAN

SPICED WALNUTS

1 cup walnut halves
1/2 cup sugar
1/4 cup water
1/2 teaspoon ground cinnamon
1/4 teaspoon salt
Dash of ground red pepper
Cooking spray

1. Preheat oven to 350°.
2. Arrange walnuts in a single layer on a baking sheet. Bake at 350° for 10 minutes or until lightly browned.
3. Combine sugar and next 4 ingredients (through red pepper) in a small saucepan. Cook, without stirring, until a candy thermometer registers 238° (about 8 minutes). Remove from heat; stir in walnuts. Pour walnut mixture onto baking sheet coated with cooking spray. Cool completely; break into small pieces. Store in an airtight container at room temperature for 1 week. Yield: 2 cups (serving size: 2 tablespoons).

CALORIES 60; **FAT** 3.4g (sat 0.3g, mono 0.8g, poly 2.2g); **PROTEIN** 0.8g; **CARB** 7.3g; **FIBER** 0.3g; **CHOL** 0mg; **IRON** 0.2mg; **SODIUM** 37mg; **CALC** 6mg

greens & vegetables

Lettuces, vegetables, and fruits are the stars of these salads. Make the most of in-season produce with recipes that will have you going back for seconds.

ARUGULA AND PEAR SALAD WITH TOASTED WALNUTS, p. 37 →

Add edible flowers to this salad, if you like; they not only add beautiful color, but also subtle flavor. Nasturtiums, for example, add a peppery bite. Find packaged edible flowers near herbs in grocery stores.

VEGETARIAN

BEETS WITH WALNUTS, GOAT CHEESE, AND BABY GREENS

6 medium beets (red and golden), about 1½ pounds
1 cup water
8 cups mixed baby salad greens
1 cup loosely packed fresh flat-leaf parsley leaves
1 tablespoon white balsamic vinegar
¼ teaspoon kosher salt
¼ teaspoon freshly ground black pepper
2 tablespoons extra-virgin olive oil
½ cup (2 ounces) crumbled goat cheese
¼ cup coarsely chopped walnuts, toasted

1. Preheat oven to 375°.
2. Leave root and 1-inch stem on beets; scrub with a brush. Place beets and 1 cup water in a 13 x 9–inch glass or ceramic baking dish; cover tightly with foil. Bake at 375° for 1 hour and 30 minutes or until tender. Cool beets slightly. Trim off roots; rub off skins. Cut beets into wedges; cool completely.
3. Place greens and parsley in a large bowl; toss. Combine vinegar, salt, and pepper, stirring with a whisk. Gradually drizzle in oil, stirring constantly with a whisk. Drizzle dressing over greens mixture; toss gently. Arrange 1 cup salad on each of 8 plates; top evenly with beets. Top each serving with 1 tablespoon cheese and 1½ teaspoons nuts. Yield: 8 servings.

CALORIES 125; **FAT** 8.2g (sat 2.4g, mono 3.3g, poly 1.9g); **PROTEIN** 4.1g; **CARB** 10.1g; **FIBER** 3.1g; **CHOL** 7mg; **IRON** 1.5mg; **SODIUM** 178mg; **CALC** 63mg

BEETS

When selecting fresh beets, buy small to medium globes with stems and leaves attached; firm, smooth skin; and no soft spots.

SUPERFAST / VEGETARIAN

ARUGULA AND PEAR SALAD WITH TOASTED WALNUTS

This salad combines the peppery bite of arugula with the sweetness of juicy pears and the earthy crunch of walnuts. If you can't find Bosc pears, Anjou or Starkrimson are also good choices for salads.

1 tablespoon minced shallots
2 tablespoons extra-virgin olive oil
2 teaspoons white wine vinegar
¼ teaspoon salt
¼ teaspoon Dijon mustard
⅛ teaspoon freshly ground black pepper
6 cups baby arugula leaves
2 Bosc pears, thinly sliced
¼ cup chopped walnuts, toasted

1. Combine first 6 ingredients in a large bowl; stir with a whisk. Add arugula and pears to bowl; toss to coat.
2. Arrange about 1½ cups salad on each of 4 plates; sprinkle each serving with 1 tablespoon walnuts. Yield: 4 servings.

CALORIES 168; **FAT** 12.5g (sat 1.5g, mono 5.7g, poly 4.6g); **PROTEIN** 2.5g; **CARB** 15.1g; **FIBER** 3g; **CHOL** 0mg; **IRON** 0.7mg; **SODIUM** 164mg; **CALC** 106mg

HOW TO

STORE & WASH GREENS

Keep lettuces crisp and fresh, or even revive them with some Salad CPR.

Store greens

■ Store leafy greens unwashed in zip-top plastic bags in the refrigerator; any added moisture will cause them to spoil more rapidly. When you're ready to use them, remove unwanted stems, and tear leaves into smaller pieces.

Clean greens

■ Leafy greens harbor sand and other debris, so you'll need to wash them thoroughly. Just running water over the leaves isn't enough to clean them, so skip the colander.

Instead, dunk greens in a large bowl, pot, or sink filled with cold water. The dirt will sink to the bottom while the greens float to the top. Remove the leaves by hand, and place them in another bowl. Pour out the water, and repeat the procedure until the water is free of debris. Finally, spin the greens in a salad spinner.

SALAD CPR

Here is a simple trick for crisping wilting greens: Soak them in ice water for a few minutes. The ice bath rehydrates their cells, and they perk right up, crisp as the day they were harvested. (Make sure to dry the greens well before using, or the dressing won't coat the leaves.) This technique will also work with herbs and limp veggies like older celery and carrots.

FRISÉE SALAD WITH PERSIMMONS, DATES, AND ALMONDS

1½ cups thinly sliced leek (about 1 large), divided
3 tablespoons water
2 tablespoons white wine vinegar
1 teaspoon extra-virgin olive oil
½ teaspoon kosher salt
1 ripe Fuyu persimmon, peeled and chopped (about 7 ounces)
6 cups frisée or bagged mâche salad greens
3 cups peeled and thinly sliced quartered ripe Fuyu persimmons (about 3)
3 tablespoons sliced almonds, toasted
8 pitted dates, chopped (about ¼ cup)

1. Place 1 tablespoon leek in a blender. Place 3 tablespoons water and next 4 ingredients (through chopped persimmon) in blender; process until smooth.
2. Combine frisée and remaining leek in a large bowl, and toss with dressing. Arrange 1 cup frisée mixture on each of 8 plates. Top each serving with about ⅓ cup sliced persimmon, about 1 teaspoon almonds, and 1½ teaspoons dates. Yield: 8 servings.

CALORIES 157; **FAT** 2g (sat 0.2g, mono 1.2g, poly 0.5g); **PROTEIN** 2.2g; **CARB** 37g; **FIBER** 6g; **CHOL** 0mg; **IRON** 1.2mg; **SODIUM** 134mg; **CALC** 57mg

PERSIMMONS

Choose squat, round Fuyu persimmons for salads; they are crisp when ripe and hold up well for slicing.

SUPERFAST / VEGETARIAN

ASPARAGUS AND SPRING GREENS SALAD WITH GORGONZOLA VINAIGRETTE

Serve alongside a nice steak or a piece of a flavorful fish, such as tuna or salmon.

6 cups water
1 pound green and white asparagus, trimmed and cut into (2-inch) pieces
2¼ teaspoons salt, divided
2 tablespoons minced shallots
2 tablespoons white balsamic vinegar
2 tablespoons extra-virgin olive oil
½ teaspoon grated lemon rind
¼ teaspoon freshly ground black pepper
½ cup (2 ounces) crumbled Gorgonzola cheese, divided
1 (5-ounce) package salad greens

1. Bring 6 cups water to a boil in a Dutch oven. Add asparagus and 2 teaspoons salt; cook asparagus in boiling water 2 minutes or until crisp-tender. Drain and rinse asparagus under cold water; drain.
2. Combine ¼ teaspoon salt, shallots, and next 4 ingredients (through pepper) in a small bowl, stirring with a whisk. Stir in ¼ cup cheese.
3. Combine asparagus and greens in a large bowl. Drizzle with vinaigrette; toss gently to coat. Sprinkle with ¼ cup cheese. Yield: 8 servings (serving size: about 1 cup).

CALORIES 77; **FAT** 5.5g (sat 1.8g, mono 3g, poly 0.5g); **PROTEIN** 3.1g; **CARB** 4g; **FIBER** 1.6g; **CHOL** 5mg; **IRON** 1.6mg; **SODIUM** 239mg; **CALC** 63mg

ASPARAGUS

Asparagus is at its peak between February and June. Look for spears with tight heads, and choose those that are about the same thickness so your asparagus cooks evenly.

VEGETARIAN

BEET AND ARUGULA SALAD WITH KEFALOTYRI

You can roast the beets up to two days in advance. For more visual appeal, use golden and red beets.

3 beets (about 1 pound)
2 tablespoons red wine vinegar
1 teaspoon extra-virgin olive oil
1/2 teaspoon salt
1/2 teaspoon freshly ground black pepper
6 cups arugula
1/4 cup (1 ounce) shaved fresh kefalotyri cheese

1. Preheat oven to 425°.
2. Leave root and 1-inch stem on beets; scrub with a brush. Place beets in a glass or ceramic baking dish; bake at 425° for 1 hour and 10 minutes or until tender. Cool; peel and cut into ¼-inch-thick slices.
3. Combine vinegar, oil, salt, and pepper, stirring with a whisk. Arrange beet slices in a single layer on a platter. Drizzle beets with half of vinegar mixture.
4. Combine remaining vinegar mixture and arugula in a large bowl; toss gently to coat. Top beets with arugula mixture. Sprinkle with cheese. Yield: 8 servings (serving size: about ½ cup beet and arugula mixture and 1½ teaspoons cheese).

CALORIES 50; **FAT** 1.8g (sat 0.7g, mono 0.7g, poly 0.2g); **PROTEIN** 2.7g; **CARB** 6.2g; **FIBER** 1.9g; **CHOL** 3mg; **IRON** 0.7mg; **SODIUM** 250mg; **CALC** 73mg

KEFALOTYRI

Kefalotyri is a hard, salty Greek cheese. Parmigiano-Reggiano can sub in a pinch.

VEGETARIAN

SPINACH WITH GARLIC VINAIGRETTE

1 1/2 tablespoons extra-virgin olive oil
1 tablespoon white wine vinegar
1/2 teaspoon Dijon mustard
1/4 teaspoon freshly ground black pepper
1/8 teaspoon salt
2 garlic cloves, minced
6 cups baby spinach leaves (about 6 ounces)
1/4 cup vertically sliced red onion

1. Combine first 6 ingredients in a large bowl, stirring well with a whisk. Add 6 cups spinach and red onion; toss to coat. Yield: 4 servings (serving size: 1¾ cups).

CALORIES 66; **FAT** 5.1g (sat 0.7g, mono 3.7g, poly 0.5g); **PROTEIN** 1.1g; **CARB** 5.2g; **FIBER** 1.9g; **CHOL** 0mg; **IRON** 1.3mg; **SODIUM** 147mg; **CALC** 31mg

SUPERFAST

BRUSSELS SPROUTS SALAD WITH WARM BACON VINAIGRETTE

3/4 pound Brussels sprouts
6 slices applewood-smoked bacon
1/3 cup white wine vinegar
1 1/2 tablespoons maple syrup
2 teaspoons Dijon mustard
1/4 teaspoon salt
1/4 teaspoon freshly ground black pepper
6 cups chopped romaine lettuce
1/4 cup coarsely chopped pecans, toasted

1. Pull leaves from Brussels sprouts, or drop Brussels sprouts through the food chute of a food processor fitted with the slicer attachment with food processor on; transfer Brussels sprouts to a bowl.
2. Heat a large nonstick skillet over medium-high heat. Add bacon to pan; cook 5 minutes or until crisp, turning occasionally. Remove bacon from pan, reserving 2 tablespoons drippings in pan; set bacon aside. Reduce heat to medium-low; add vinegar and next 4 ingredients (through pepper), stirring well to combine. Add Brussels sprouts; cook 1 minute, stirring to coat. Cover and cook 2 minutes. Combine Brussels sprouts mixture and lettuce in a large bowl; toss until well combined. Sprinkle evenly with bacon and pecans. Serve immediately. Yield: 8 servings (serving size: 1 cup).

CALORIES 120; **FAT** 8.6g (sat 2.5g, mono 4.2g, poly 1.7g); **PROTEIN** 3.8g; **CARB** 7.7g; **FIBER** 2.3g; **CHOL** 9mg; **IRON** 1mg; **SODIUM** 223mg; **CALC** 35mg

BRUSSELS SPROUTS

A member of the cabbage family, Brussels sprouts are at their best between September and February. Look for small, firm sprouts with compact, bright-green heads—the smaller the head, the sweeter the taste. Try to choose sprouts of similar size so they'll cook evenly.

NUTS ABOUT IT

Looking for a little more crunch in your salad? Nuts and seeds add texture, flavor, and a nutrition boost, too. One-fourth cup of nuts or seeds adds nearly five grams of high-quality protein, as well as generous amounts of vitamin E, fiber, minerals, and arginine, a compound that helps blood vessels to function. Nuts and seeds are high in fat—the healthful, unsaturated kind.

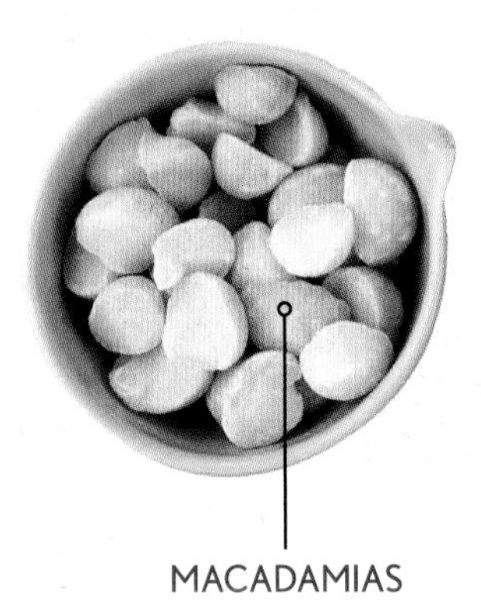

CANDIED WALNUT, PEAR, AND LEAFY GREEN SALAD

1/3 cup sugar
2/3 cup chopped walnuts, toasted
Cooking spray
1/2 teaspoon kosher salt, divided
2 tablespoons white balsamic vinegar
1 1/2 teaspoons Dijon mustard
3 tablespoons extra-virgin olive oil
1 tablespoon capers, chopped
4 cups torn green leaf lettuce
4 cups chopped romaine lettuce
4 cups chopped radicchio
1 ripe red Anjou pear, thinly sliced
1/4 teaspoon freshly ground black pepper

1. Place sugar in a small, heavy saucepan over medium-high heat; cook until sugar dissolves, stirring gently as needed to dissolve sugar evenly (about 1 minute). Continue cooking 1 minute or until golden (do not stir). Remove from heat; carefully stir in nuts to coat evenly. Spread nuts on a baking sheet coated with cooking spray; separate nuts quickly. Sprinkle with ¼ teaspoon salt. Set aside until cool; break into small pieces.
2. Combine vinegar and mustard, stirring with a whisk. Gradually add oil, stirring constantly with a whisk. Stir in capers.
3. Combine lettuces and radicchio; top with pear and candied walnuts. Drizzle dressing evenly over salad; sprinkle with ¼ teaspoon salt and pepper. Toss gently to combine.
Yield: 8 servings (serving size: about 1 cup).

CALORIES 171; **FAT** 11.6g (sat 1.3g, mono 4.6g, poly 5.2g); **PROTEIN** 2.7g; **CARB** 16.3g; **FIBER** 2.6g; **CHOL** 0mg; **IRON** 1mg; **SODIUM** 177mg; **CALC** 37mg

MAKE-AHEAD / VEGETARIAN

CHARRED VEGETABLE SALAD

Although you can successfully prepare this colorful end-of-summer salad on a gas grill, charcoal will imbue the vegetables with extra flavor. White wine vinegar can stand in for the champagne vinegar without compromising the flavor of the dish.

2 red bell peppers, halved and seeded
1½ pounds eggplant, cut into (½-inch-thick) slices (about 2 medium)
1 sweet onion, cut into 8 wedges
2 cups cherry tomatoes
½ teaspoon freshly ground black pepper, divided
3 tablespoons extra-virgin olive oil, divided
¾ teaspoon salt, divided
Cooking spray
1 tablespoon champagne or white wine vinegar
½ teaspoon sugar
2 garlic cloves, minced
1 ounce oil-cured olives (about 12), pitted and halved
¼ cup fresh small basil leaves
1 tablespoon finely chopped fresh chives

1. Preheat grill to medium-high heat.
2. Combine first 4 ingredients, ¼ teaspoon black pepper, 1 tablespoon oil, and ¼ teaspoon salt. Place bell peppers, skin sides down, and onion on grill rack coated with cooking spray; grill 10 minutes. Turn onion; add eggplant to grill. Remove bell peppers. Place bell peppers in a zip-top plastic bag; seal. Let stand 10 minutes. Grill eggplant and onion 5 minutes; remove onion. Turn eggplant; grill 5 minutes. Remove eggplant. Add tomatoes to a grill basket; grill 5 minutes. Remove bell peppers from bag. Peel and discard skins; slice lengthwise.
3. Combine ¼ teaspoon salt, vinegar, and sugar. Slowly add 2 tablespoons oil, stirring with a whisk. Combine vegetables, dressing, garlic, and olives. Sprinkle with ¼ teaspoon salt, ¼ teaspoon black pepper, basil, and chives. Yield: 8 servings (serving size: about ¾ cup).

CALORIES 99; **FAT** 5.9g (sat 0.8g, mono 4g, poly 0.8g); **PROTEIN** 2g; **CARB** 11.7g; **FIBER** 4.7g; **CHOL** 0mg; **IRON** 0.9mg; **SODIUM** 258mg; **CALC** 23mg

MAKE-AHEAD / PORTABLE / VEGETARIAN

CELERY AND PARSLEY SALAD WITH GOLDEN RAISINS ➤

A perfect complement to a heavy entrée, consider putting this on the table with a holiday meal.

¼ cup golden raisins
2½ tablespoons white balsamic vinegar
2⅓ cups thinly diagonally sliced celery (including leaves)
1⅓ cups loosely packed fresh flat-leaf parsley leaves
¼ teaspoon kosher salt
¼ teaspoon freshly ground black pepper
4 teaspoons extra-virgin olive oil

1. Combine raisins and vinegar in a small microwave-safe bowl; microwave at HIGH 1 minute and 15 seconds or until raisins are plump. Drain raisins in a sieve over a medium bowl, reserving 1 tablespoon vinegar; discard remaining vinegar.
2. Combine raisins, celery, and parsley in a large bowl.
3. Add salt and pepper to reserved vinegar, stirring with a whisk. Gradually add oil, stirring constantly with a whisk. Drizzle dressing over salad; toss gently to coat. Yield: 4 servings (serving size: about ⅔ cup).

CALORIES 87; **FAT** 5g (sat 0.7g, mono 3.4g, poly 0.8g); **PROTEIN** 1.4g; **CARB** 11g; **FIBER** 2g; **CHOL** 0mg; **IRON** 1.5mg; **SODIUM** 191mg; **CALC** 60mg

KID-FRIENDLY / MAKE-AHEAD / PORTABLE / VEGETARIAN

CREAMY BUTTERMILK-HERB POTATO SALAD

Make sure the potatoes cook until just tender and no more; that way, they'll hold their shape.

3 pounds small red potatoes, quartered
1/2 cup crème fraîche or sour cream
1/3 cup nonfat buttermilk
1/4 cup chopped fresh parsley
2 tablespoons chopped fresh chives
1 tablespoon chopped fresh dill
1 1/4 teaspoons kosher salt
1/2 teaspoon freshly ground black pepper
1 large garlic clove, minced
Dill sprigs (optional)

1. Place potatoes in a Dutch oven, and cover with water. Bring to a boil. Reduce heat, and simmer 15 minutes or until just tender; drain. Cool 30 minutes.

2. Combine crème fraîche and next 7 ingredients (through garlic) in a large bowl; stir with a whisk. Add warm potatoes; toss gently to coat. Garnish with dill sprigs, if desired. Serve at room temperature or chilled. Yield: 8 servings (serving size: about 1 cup).

CALORIES 176; **FAT** 5.5g (sat 3.3g, mono 1.5g, poly 0.3g); **PROTEIN** 4.1g; **CARB** 28g; **FIBER** 3g; **CHOL** 14mg; **IRON** 1.4mg; **SODIUM** 326mg; **CALC** 34mg

CRÈME FRAÎCHE

A thickened cream product with a mild, tangy, nutty flavor, crème fraîche is available in tubs near the gourmet cheeses. If you can't find it, substitute full-fat sour cream.

MAKE-AHEAD / PORTABLE / VEGETARIAN

FARMERS' MARKET POTATO SALAD

Look for a mix of red, purple, and brown-skinned fingerling potatoes, so named because of their oblong shapes, for this stunning salad. If you can't find them, substitute small red potatoes. You can serve this dish at room temperature just after it's tossed together, or make it ahead, refrigerate, and serve chilled.

1 cup fresh corn kernels (about 2 ears)
2 pounds fingerling potatoes, cut into 1-inch pieces
2½ tablespoons olive oil, divided
2 tablespoons chopped fresh tarragon
2 tablespoons cider vinegar
2 tablespoons whole-grain Dijon mustard
½ teaspoon hot pepper sauce
¼ teaspoon salt
½ teaspoon freshly ground black pepper
Cooking spray
¾ cup vertically sliced red onion
¾ cup diced zucchini
1 cup cherry tomatoes, halved

1. Preheat oven to 425°.
2. Place corn and potatoes on a jelly-roll pan. Drizzle vegetables with 1 tablespoon oil; toss to coat. Bake at 425° for 30 minutes or until potatoes are tender. Place mixture in a large bowl. Combine tarragon and next 5 ingredients (through pepper) in a small bowl, stirring with a whisk. Gradually add 1½ tablespoons oil, stirring constantly with a whisk. Drizzle dressing over potato mixture; toss gently to coat.
3. Heat a large skillet over medium heat. Coat pan with cooking spray. Add onion and zucchini to pan; cook 4 minutes or until lightly browned, stirring occasionally. Add zucchini mixture and tomatoes to potato mixture; toss gently to combine. Yield: 8 servings (serving size: about ¾ cup).

CALORIES 152; **FAT** 5.2g (sat 0.7g, mono 3.2g, poly 0.8g); **PROTEIN** 3.3g; **CARB** 24.8g; **FIBER** 3g; **CHOL** 0mg; **IRON** 1.1mg; **SODIUM** 192mg; **CALC** 21mg

MAKE-AHEAD / VEGETARIAN

FENNEL SALAD WITH LEMON

This simple, refreshing salad would be a nice complement to a fish dinner.

¼ cup coarsely chopped fresh parsley
2 fennel bulbs, trimmed, halved, and cut into thin vertical slices
1 shallot, halved and cut into thin vertical slices
2 tablespoons extra-virgin olive oil
1 teaspoon sugar
½ teaspoon kosher salt
¼ teaspoon freshly ground black pepper
⅔ cup Meyer lemon sections (about 3 lemons)
2 ounces goat cheese, cut into 6 slices

1. Combine first 3 ingredients in a bowl. Drizzle mixture with oil; sprinkle with sugar, salt, and pepper. Toss. Add lemon sections; toss gently to combine. Cover and chill 1 hour. Top with cheese. Yield: 6 servings (serving size: 1 cup salad and 1 cheese slice).

CALORIES 107; **FAT** 6.9g (sat 2.1g, mono 3.8g, poly 0.8g); **PROTEIN** 3.3g; **CARB** 10.5g; **FIBER** 3.3g; **CHOL** 4mg; **IRON** 1.2mg; **SODIUM** 238mg; **CALC** 65mg

FIGS

Figs, which are actually inverted flowers, have a short season, from June to October. Since fresh figs have delicate skins, you should use them as soon as possible. They can last up to five days in the refrigerator.

SUPERFAST / VEGETARIAN

FIG, TOMATO, AND SWEET ONION SALAD

For this recipe, any fig variety you like or a combination of varieties will work.

2 tablespoons red wine vinegar
2 teaspoons extra-virgin olive oil
¼ teaspoon freshly ground black pepper
2 cups quartered fresh figs (about ½ pound)
2 cups torn romaine lettuce
1 cup cherry tomatoes, halved
¾ cup vertically sliced Vidalia or other sweet onion
3 tablespoons chopped fresh mint
¼ cup (1 ounce) crumbled feta cheese

1. Combine first 3 ingredients in a large bowl; stir well with a whisk. Add figs, lettuce, tomatoes, onion, and mint; toss gently to coat. Sprinkle with cheese. Yield: 4 servings (serving size: 1½ cups).

CALORIES 128; **FAT** 4.8g (sat 1.8g, mono 2.2g, poly 0.6g); **PROTEIN** 3.4g; **CARB** 20.1g; **FIBER** 4.2g; **CHOL** 8mg; **IRON** 1.5mg; **SODIUM** 114mg; **CALC** 105mg

SUPERFAST / VEGETARIAN

FRESH ENGLISH PEA SALAD WITH MINT AND PECORINO

This simple salad boasts plenty of early summer flavor. You can substitute crumbled feta cheese for the pecorino. If you can't find fresh peas, use frozen thawed petite green peas.

4 cups water
1 cup shelled green peas (about 1 pound unshelled)
6 cups trimmed arugula
1/4 cup chopped fresh mint
1 1/2 tablespoons fresh lemon juice
1 tablespoon extra-virgin olive oil
1/2 teaspoon salt
1/4 teaspoon freshly ground black pepper
1/2 cup (2 ounces) shaved fresh pecorino Romano cheese

1. Bring 4 cups water to a boil in a medium saucepan. Add peas; cook 1 minute. Drain and plunge peas into ice water; drain.
2. Combine peas, arugula, and mint in a large bowl. Add lemon juice, olive oil, salt, and pepper; toss well. Sprinkle with cheese. Serve immediately. Yield: 8 servings (serving size: about 1 cup salad and 1 tablespoon cheese).

CALORIES 90; **FAT** 4g (sat 1.3g, mono 1.4g, poly 0.2g); **PROTEIN** 5.6g; **CARB** 9.1g; **FIBER** 3.3g; **CHOL** 6mg; **IRON** 1.1mg; **SODIUM** 342mg; **CALC** 107mg

GREEN PEAS

One of spring's finest pleasures, fresh green peas (or English peas) lend an unmistakable starchy, grassy sweetness to any dish.

SUPERFAST / VEGETARIAN

FRISÉE AND ARUGULA SALAD

1/4 cup canola mayonnaise
1 tablespoon chopped fresh dill
2 tablespoons water
1 tablespoon sherry vinegar
1 1/2 teaspoons Dijon mustard
1/2 teaspoon freshly ground black pepper
1/4 teaspoon salt
2 cups frisée
2 cups baby arugula
1/2 cup thinly sliced fennel bulb
1/2 cup thinly sliced cucumber
1/2 cup thinly sliced radishes
2 tablespoons pine nuts, toasted

1. Combine first 7 ingredients in a large bowl; stir with a whisk. Add frisée, baby arugula, fennel bulb, cucumber, and radishes. Toss gently to combine. Divide salad evenly among 4 plates; sprinkle each salad with ½ tablespoon toasted pine nuts. Yield: 4 servings.

CALORIES 147; **FAT** 14.1g (sat 0.7g, mono 4.3g, poly 8.5g); **PROTEIN** 1.5g; **CARB** 4.1g; **FIBER** 1.8g; **CHOL** 5mg; **IRON** 0.8mg; **SODIUM** 303mg; **CALC** 42mg

RADISHES

In the fullness of spring, radishes are at their peak and quite mild. (Radishes harvested in the summer heat have a much sharper, almost biting taste.) Interesting heirloom varieties abound in farmers' markets. Look for bunches of radishes with the leaves still attached; the greens are a guarantee of the roots' freshness.

ESCAROLE

Taste: Like its relative, Belgian endive, it's slightly bitter. Choose young, tender leaves for raw salads.

Smart substitutions: mesclun, mustard greens, arugula, or spinach

FRISÉE

Taste: Also known as curly endive, these lacy greens are slightly bitter.

Smart substitutions: a salad blend with frisée or radicchio. Pea shoots and mâche have sweeter flavor but will add similar body to a salad.

WATERCRESS

Taste: A member of the mustard family, it's peppery, with a touch of mustard.

Smart substitution: arugula

BELGIAN ENDIVE

Taste: It has a slightly bitter taste and a prickly texture.

Smart substitutions: escarole, mustard greens, arugula, or spinach

SPINACH

Taste: It's mildly bitter and earthy.

Smart substitution: arugula

ARUGULA

Taste: This pleasantly pungent and peppery green is also known as rocket, roquette, rugula, and rucola. It is a staple of Italian fare and often found in mesclun (young tender greens) salad mixes, where it behaves like a cross between lettuce and herb.

Smart substitutions: watercress, endive, or young mustard greens

SUPERFAST / VEGETARIAN

ASIAN SNAP PEA SALAD WITH SESAME-ORANGE DRESSING

Dressing:

1 large orange
1 tablespoon rice vinegar
2 teaspoons lower-sodium soy sauce
1½ teaspoons dark sesame oil
1 teaspoon brown sugar
1 teaspoon Sriracha (hot chile sauce)

Salad:

2 teaspoons canola oil
1½ cups thinly sliced red bell pepper
¾ cup thinly sliced carrot
12 ounces sugar snap peas, trimmed
¼ teaspoon kosher salt
½ cup diagonally cut green onions
1 (6-ounce) package fresh baby spinach
1 teaspoon sesame seeds, toasted

1. To prepare dressing, grate 1 teaspoon orange rind; squeeze ⅓ cup juice from orange over a bowl. Set rind aside. Combine juice, vinegar, and next 4 ingredients (through chile sauce) in a small bowl; stir with a whisk.

2. To prepare salad, heat 2 teaspoons canola oil in a large nonstick skillet over medium-high heat. Add bell pepper and carrot to pan; sauté 1 minute, stirring occasionally. Add reserved orange rind, sugar snap peas, and salt to pan; sauté 2 minutes, stirring occasionally. Transfer pea mixture to a large bowl; cool 5 minutes. Stir in green onions and spinach. Pour dressing over salad; toss gently to coat. Sprinkle with sesame seeds. Serve immediately. Yield: 6 servings (serving size: 1⅓ cups).

CALORIES 89; **FAT** 3.2g (sat 0.4g, mono 1.6g, poly 1.1g); **PROTEIN** 2.9g; **CARB** 13.3g; **FIBER** 4.2g; **CHOL** 0mg; **IRON** 2.5mg; **SODIUM** 218mg; **CALC** 66mg

VEGETARIAN

GOLDEN CORN SALAD WITH FRESH BASIL

Give yourself a head start on this salad by cooking the potatoes a day ahead.

8 ounces small yellow Finnish potatoes or small red potatoes
3 cups fresh corn kernels (about 4 ears)
2 cups assorted tear-drop cherry tomatoes (pear-shaped), halved
1½ cups chopped red bell pepper
¼ cup minced shallots
3 tablespoons white balsamic vinegar
1 tablespoon Dijon mustard
½ teaspoon kosher salt
¼ teaspoon freshly ground black pepper
3 tablespoons extra-virgin olive oil
6 cups arugula, trimmed
½ cup torn fresh basil leaves
2 ounces goat cheese, sliced

1. Place potatoes in a small saucepan; cover with water. Bring to a boil; cook 11 minutes or until tender. Drain and chill. Cut potatoes in half lengthwise. Combine potatoes, corn, tomatoes, and bell pepper in a large bowl.

2. Combine shallots and next 4 ingredients (through black pepper) in a small bowl, stirring with a whisk. Slowly pour oil into shallot mixture, stirring constantly with a whisk. Drizzle over corn mixture; toss well. Add arugula; toss. Sprinkle with basil; top evenly with goat cheese. Yield: 4 servings (serving size: 2¼ cups).

CALORIES 337; **FAT** 16.5g (sat 4.7g, mono 8.9g, poly 2.4g); **PROTEIN** 10g; **CARB** 43.2g; **FIBER** 6.8g; **CHOL** 11mg; **IRON** 2.2mg; **SODIUM** 376mg; **CALC** 131mg

CORN

Fresh summer sweet corn is a treat. Corn begins to lose its sweetness quickly after it's picked, so try to find corn that was picked the same day you buy it. Look for tight, green husks and golden, moist silks.

KID-FRIENDLY / PORTABLE / VEGETARIAN

GRILLED ROMAINE WITH CREAMY HERB DRESSING

A brief turn over hot coals wilts hearty romaine lettuce ever so slightly and infuses it with a delicious smoky flavor, yielding a special salad that's easy to put together. Serve with any type of grilled meat, fish, or burgers.

1 large head romaine lettuce, trimmed and halved lengthwise
2 teaspoons olive oil
Cooking spray
½ teaspoon freshly ground black pepper, divided
⅜ teaspoon salt, divided
¼ cup canola mayonnaise
1½ teaspoons chopped fresh dill
1 tablespoon chopped fresh flat-leaf parsley
2 tablespoons fresh lemon juice
1 tablespoon water
2 garlic cloves, minced

1. Preheat grill to medium-high heat.
2. Brush cut sides of lettuce evenly with oil. Place lettuce, cut sides down, on grill rack coated with cooking spray, and grill 2 minutes. Remove from heat; cut each lettuce half lengthwise in half again to form 4 quarters. Sprinkle cut sides of lettuce with ¼ teaspoon black pepper and ⅛ teaspoon salt.
3. Combine ¼ teaspoon pepper, ¼ teaspoon salt, mayonnaise, and next 5 ingredients (through garlic) in a small bowl, stirring well. Arrange 1 lettuce quarter on each of 4 plates; drizzle each serving with about 4 teaspoons dressing. Serve immediately. Yield: 4 servings.

CALORIES 132; **FAT** 13.4g (sat 1.3g, mono 7.7g, poly 3.3g); **PROTEIN** 0.7g; **CARB** 2.7g; **FIBER** 1g; **CHOL** 5mg; **IRON** 0.5mg; **SODIUM** 325mg; **CALC** 19mg

SUPERFAST / VEGETARIAN

GREEN SALAD WITH HAZELNUT VINAIGRETTE

Be sure your oil smells nutty and has not gone rancid. Toasted nut oils offer more flavor than oils made from raw nuts. You can replace the hazelnut oil with other nut oils, such as toasted pecan, toasted walnut, or toasted pistachio.

1½ teaspoons red wine vinegar
¼ teaspoon Dijon mustard
⅛ teaspoon fine sea salt
⅛ teaspoon freshly ground black pepper
1½ tablespoons toasted hazelnut oil
4 cups packaged herb salad blend
½ shallot, thinly sliced

1. Combine first 4 ingredients in a large bowl, stirring with a whisk. Gradually add oil to vinegar mixture, stirring constantly with a whisk. Add salad blend and shallot, tossing to coat. Serve immediately. Yield: 4 servings (serving size: about 1 cup).

CALORIES 59; **FAT** 5.2g (sat 0.4g, mono 4g, poly 0.6g); **PROTEIN** 1g; **CARB** 2.6g; **FIBER** 1.2g; **CHOL** 0mg; **IRON** 0.8mg; **SODIUM** 94mg; **CALC** 32mg

SUPERFAST / VEGETARIAN

HONEY BALSAMIC-ARUGULA SALAD

The flavor from the vinaigrette elevates this salad from humble to outstanding. If you have time, toast the walnuts and allow them to cool for more flavor.

2 tablespoons balsamic vinegar
2 tablespoons olive oil
1 tablespoon minced shallots
1 tablespoon chopped fresh parsley
1 teaspoon Dijon mustard
1 teaspoon honey
1/8 teaspoon salt
1/4 teaspoon freshly ground black pepper
1 garlic clove, crushed
6 cups arugula
1/4 cup sliced red onion
1/4 cup shaved Parmesan
2 tablespoons chopped walnuts

1. Combine first 9 ingredients in a large bowl; stir well with a whisk. Add arugula, onion, Parmesan, and walnuts; toss gently to coat. Divide salad evenly among 4 plates. Yield: 4 servings.

CALORIES 140; **FAT** 11.6g (sat 2.4g, mono 5.4g, poly 2.8g); **PROTEIN** 3.9g; **CARB** 6.4g; **FIBER** 0.9g; **CHOL** 6mg; **IRON** 0.7mg; **SODIUM** 215mg; **CALC** 135mg

MAKE-AHEAD / VEGETARIAN

JALAPEÑO-LIME SLAW ➤

Fresh and pleasantly spicy, this citrusy take on coleslaw is an ideal side dish or topping for bratwursts or burgers. Leave the seeds in some peppers for added fire, or seed all of them for a milder dish.

1/3 cup fresh lime juice
1 teaspoon sugar
3/4 teaspoon kosher salt
1/4 teaspoon freshly ground black pepper
3 tablespoons olive oil
1/2 cup thinly vertically sliced red onion
1/2 cup coarsely chopped fresh cilantro
1 (16-ounce) package cabbage-and-carrot coleslaw
4 jalapeño peppers, divided

1. Combine first 4 ingredients in a large bowl, stirring with a whisk. Gradually add olive oil, stirring constantly with a whisk. Add onion, cilantro, and coleslaw. **2.** Cut 1 jalapeño pepper in half crosswise; remove seeds from 1 pepper half. Cut both halves crosswise into thin slices. Cut 3 jalapeño peppers in half crosswise. Remove seeds from halves, and cut crosswise into thin slices. Add jalapeños to onion mixture, and toss well to coat. Cover and chill at least 1 hour. Yield: 8 servings (serving size: about ¾ cup).

CALORIES 71; **FAT** 5.2g (sat 0.7g, mono 3.7g, poly 0.6g); **PROTEIN** 0.9g; **CARB** 6.3g; **FIBER** 1.8g; **CHOL** 0mg; **IRON** 0.4mg; **SODIUM** 198mg; **CALC** 26mg

MAKE-AHEAD / PORTABLE / VEGETARIAN

LEMON-ARUGULA POTATO SALAD

This potato salad is a nice accompaniment to barbecued meat; the lemony flavor brings balance to rich flavors. If you want to make the potato salad ahead, prepare the recipe through Step 2. Once the potato mixture is completely cooled, cover and refrigerate. Planning to take it to an event? Pack the dressed potatoes and the arugula separately, and keep the arugula cool. Toss with fresh arugula just before serving so the greens don't wilt or get bruised.

2 pounds Yukon gold potatoes, peeled and cut into 1-inch pieces
7 teaspoons extra-virgin olive oil, divided
1/2 cup finely chopped shallots (about 3 small)
1 1/2 tablespoons sherry vinegar
2 teaspoons stone-ground mustard
1 teaspoon grated lemon rind
1 teaspoon fresh lemon juice
3/8 teaspoon salt
1/4 teaspoon freshly ground black pepper
2 1/2 cups loosely packed arugula

1. Place potato pieces in a medium saucepan; cover with cold water to 2 inches above potatoes. Bring to a boil over medium-high heat. Reduce heat to medium, and gently simmer 10 minutes or until potatoes are tender. Drain potatoes.

2. Heat a small skillet over medium-high heat. Add 1 teaspoon oil to pan; swirl to coat. Add shallots to pan; sauté 3 minutes or until lightly browned, stirring occasionally. Remove from heat. Combine shallots, vinegar, and next 5 ingredients (through black pepper) in a small bowl, stirring well with a whisk. Gradually add 2 tablespoons oil, stirring constantly with a whisk. Drizzle dressing over warm potatoes; toss gently to coat. Cool completely.

3. Add arugula to potato mixture; toss gently. Serve immediately. Yield: 6 servings (serving size: about 1 cup).

CALORIES 155; **FAT** 5.3g (sat 0.7g, mono 3.8g, poly 0.6g); **PROTEIN** 3.2g; **CARB** 23.1g; **FIBER** 1.6g; **CHOL** 0mg; **IRON** 1.3mg; **SODIUM** 173mg; **CALC** 19mg

POTATOES

For salads, waxy or all-purpose instead of starchy potatoes are best. The Yukon gold is an all-purpose potato that will maintain its shape after being boiled. Other good salad potatoes include red-skinned, purple, Yellow Finn, and white round potatoes, as well as fingerlings.

MAKE-AHEAD / PORTABLE / VEGETARIAN

LEMONY CUCUMBER SALAD

Something fresh, vibrant, and crunchy is often missing from potluck gatherings; this easy salad will get gobbled up quickly because it satisfies on all those levels.

1 cup thinly sliced radishes
1/2 cup finely chopped orange bell pepper
1/4 cup chopped fresh flat-leaf parsley
2 English cucumbers, thinly sliced (about 6 cups)
1 teaspoon finely grated lemon rind
2 tablespoons fresh lemon juice
1 tablespoon extra-virgin olive oil
1 1/2 teaspoons white wine vinegar
1/2 teaspoon salt
1/4 teaspoon freshly ground black pepper

1. Combine first 4 ingredients in a large bowl.
2. Combine lemon rind and next 5 ingredients (through black pepper) in a small bowl, stirring with a whisk. Pour dressing over cucumber mixture; toss well to coat. Serve at room temperature or chilled. Yield: 8 servings (serving size: 2/3 cup).

CALORIES 33; **FAT** 1.8g (sat 0.3g, mono 1.2g, poly 0.2g); **PROTEIN** 0.8g; **CARB** 4.3g; **FIBER** 0.9g; **CHOL** 0mg; **IRON** 0.4mg; **SODIUM** 156mg; **CALC** 20mg

ENGLISH CUCUMBERS

Virtually seedless, hothouse or English cucumbers offer a sweet advantage when you want to avoid bitter seeds in other varieties.

MAKE-AHEAD / PORTABLE / VEGETARIAN

MARKET SALAD WITH GOAT CHEESE AND CHAMPAGNE-SHALLOT VINAIGRETTE

Fresh herbs make all the difference in this versatile dressing. Try it on any combination of greens and vegetables from your local farmers' market.

2 medium beets (about 3/4 pound)
8 ounces green beans, trimmed and cut into 2-inch pieces
1 (15-ounce) can no-salt-added chickpeas (garbanzo beans), rinsed and drained
3 tablespoons finely chopped shallots
2 tablespoons chopped fresh mint
1 tablespoon chopped fresh tarragon
3 tablespoons walnut or olive oil
2 tablespoons champagne or white wine vinegar
1 tablespoon fresh lemon juice
1 1/2 teaspoons Dijon mustard
1/4 teaspoon salt
1/8 teaspoon freshly ground black pepper
2 medium heirloom tomatoes, each cut into 8 wedges
1/2 cup (2 ounces) crumbled goat cheese

1. Preheat oven to 350°.
2. Leave root and 1-inch stem on beets; scrub with a brush. Wrap beets in heavy-duty foil. Bake at 350° for 1 hour and 15 minutes or until tender. Remove from oven; cool. Trim off beet roots and stems; rub off skins. Cut each beet into 8 wedges.
3. Cook beans in boiling water 4 minutes or until crisp-tender. Drain and plunge beans into ice water; drain well. Combine beans and chickpeas in a medium bowl.
4. Combine shallots and next 8 ingredients (through pepper) in a small bowl, stirring with a whisk. Add 2 tablespoons vinaigrette to beets; toss well. Combine 2 tablespoons vinaigrette and tomatoes in a bowl; toss gently to coat. Add remaining vinaigrette to bean mixture, tossing well to combine. Arrange ¾ cup bean mixture on each of 4 plates. Arrange 4 pieces each of beets and tomatoes around bean mixture. Sprinkle each serving with 2 tablespoons cheese. Yield: 4 servings.

CALORIES 345; **FAT** 15.8g (sat 3.9g, mono 3.4g, poly 6.8g); **PROTEIN** 13g; **CARB** 40.1g; **FIBER** 10.5g; **CHOL** 11mg; **IRON** 3.2mg; **SODIUM** 370mg; **CALC** 161mg

TARRAGON

Tarragon has long, pointed leaves and an intense, aniselike flavor. Use it sparingly; a little goes a long way.

KID-FRIENDLY / MAKE-AHEAD / PORTABLE / SUPERFAST / VEGETARIAN

NEW-FASHIONED APPLE AND RAISIN SLAW

Crunchy, creamy, sweet, and a bit spicy, this slaw has all the elements to become a family favorite.

1/2 cup light sour cream
3 tablespoons reduced-fat mayonnaise
1 1/2 tablespoons white balsamic vinegar
1 teaspoon sugar
1/2 teaspoon freshly ground black pepper
1/4 teaspoon salt
2 cups unpeeled chopped Rome apple (about 1 medium)
1 cup golden raisins
1 (16-ounce) package cabbage-and-carrot coleslaw

1. Combine first 6 ingredients in a large bowl, stirring with a whisk.
2. Add chopped apple, 1 cup raisins, and coleslaw; toss to combine. Yield: 8 servings (serving size: 1 cup).

CALORIES 120; **FAT** 2.2g (sat 1.2g, mono 0.8g, poly 0.2g); **PROTEIN** 2.3g; **CARB** 25.3g; **FIBER** 3.3g; **CHOL** 0mg; **IRON** 0.8mg; **SODIUM** 162mg; **CALC** 31mg

APPLES

For salads, choose Rome or other crisp varieties of apples, such as Cortland or Ginger Gold, that resist browning when cut.

MAKE-AHEAD / SUPERFAST / VEGETARIAN

ORANGE SALAD WITH ARUGULA AND OIL-CURED OLIVES

Serve this minty salad as a first course for a holiday feast. You can prepare every component well in advance. Make the dressing several hours or even a day ahead; just bring to room temperature before tossing with the arugula. Buy washed and ready-to-use arugula. It takes time to peel and slice the oranges, so do that ahead, arranging the oranges on a plate and covering with plastic wrap. If you can find fresh blood oranges, they make a stunning presentation.

Dressing:

1/3 cup thinly sliced shallots
1/4 cup fresh lemon juice
2 tablespoons finely chopped fresh mint leaves
1 teaspoon sugar
2 teaspoons Dijon mustard
1/4 teaspoon kosher salt
1/8 teaspoon freshly ground black pepper
1/4 cup extra-virgin olive oil

Salad:

1 (5-ounce) package arugula
5 oranges, peeled and thinly sliced crosswise
30 oil-cured black olives
Freshly ground black pepper (optional)

1. To prepare dressing, combine first 7 ingredients in a medium bowl, stirring with a whisk. Gradually add oil, stirring constantly with a whisk.

2. To prepare salad, combine arugula and three-fourths of dressing in a large bowl; toss gently to coat. Arrange about ½ cup arugula mixture on each of 10 plates; arrange orange slices evenly over salads. Drizzle remaining dressing evenly over salads; top each salad with 3 olives. Sprinkle evenly with black pepper, if desired. Serve immediately. Yield: 10 servings.

CALORIES 117; **FAT** 8.1g (sat 1.2g, mono 5.7g, poly 1.1g); **PROTEIN** 1.2g; **CARB** 11.3g; **FIBER** 1.9g; **CHOL** 0mg; **IRON** 0.4mg; **SODIUM** 279mg; **CALC** 52mg

ORANGES

Try different varieties of oranges for their color and flavor twists. Ruby-fleshed blood oranges, with a raspberry-like flavor, are available December through May. Pink-colored Cara Cara oranges, available from December through April, are sweeter.

VEGETARIAN

PEA SHOOT SALAD WITH RADISHES AND PICKLED ONION

With a faint pea flavor, pea shoots are lovely in salads, stir-fries, pizzas, and soups. Look for them at farm stands or Asian markets in spring, and get them while you can—their flavor turns bitter at the end of the growing season.

1 cup cider vinegar
½ cup water
½ teaspoon sugar
¾ cup thinly vertically sliced red onion
4 cups water
1 cup shelled fresh English peas
1 teaspoon salt
6 cups pea shoots
10 radishes, thinly sliced
2 tablespoons extra-virgin olive oil
1½ tablespoons white wine vinegar
¼ teaspoon salt
¼ teaspoon freshly ground black pepper

1. Combine cider vinegar, ½ cup water, and sugar, stirring until sugar dissolves. Add onion; let stand 30 minutes. Drain.
2. Bring 4 cups water to a boil; add English peas and 1 teaspoon salt. Cook 2 minutes. Drain; rinse peas with cold water.
3. Combine onion, peas, pea shoots, and sliced radishes in a large bowl. Combine olive oil, white wine vinegar, ¼ teaspoon salt, and pepper in a small bowl. Drizzle oil mixture over pea mixture; toss gently. Yield: 6 servings (serving size: 1 cup).

CALORIES 87; **FAT** 3.6g (sat 0.5g, mono 2.5g, poly 0.6g); **PROTEIN** 3.5g; **CARB** 11.2g; **FIBER** 3.6g; **CHOL** 6mg; **IRON** 1.5mg; **SODIUM** 221mg; **CALC** 32mg

VEGETARIAN

PICKLED ONION, BLUE CHEESE, AND BERRY SALAD

¼ cup water
¼ cup sherry vinegar, divided
4 teaspoons agave nectar, divided
⅔ cup thinly vertically sliced Vidalia onion
1 teaspoon Dijon mustard
¼ teaspoon freshly ground black pepper
⅛ teaspoon salt
3 tablespoons extra-virgin olive oil
2 (4-ounce) packages baby mixed herb salad
½ cup (2 ounces) crumbled blue cheese
1 (6-ounce) package fresh raspberries

1. Combine ¼ cup water, 2 tablespoons vinegar, and 1 tablespoon agave in a small bowl. Add onion; toss to coat. Marinate at room temperature 30 minutes; drain.
2. Combine 2 tablespoons vinegar, 1 teaspoon agave, mustard, pepper, and salt in a large bowl, stirring with a whisk. Gradually add oil, stirring constantly with a whisk. Add salad greens; toss gently to coat. Arrange about 1 cup salad on each of 8 plates. Top each serving with about 1 tablespoon onion, 1 tablespoon cheese, and about 6 raspberries. Yield: 8 servings.

CALORIES 101; **FAT** 7.6g (sat 2.3g, mono 4.4g, poly 0.7g); **PROTEIN** 2.6g; **CARB** 6.7g; **FIBER** 2.3g; **CHOL** 6mg; **IRON** 0.5mg; **SODIUM** 180mg; **CALC** 53mg

VEGETARIAN

RADICCHIO, HARICOTS VERTS, AND SWEET LETTUCE SALAD

Bitter radicchio, balanced by prosciutto, and walnut oil, finds a place in this well-rounded salad that features all five major tastes: sweet, sour, bitter, salty, and umami. Substitute extra-virgin olive oil for walnut oil, if you prefer.

2 quarts water
2 cups (2-inch) cut haricots verts
1 tablespoon walnut oil
1 tablespoon balsamic vinegar
2 teaspoons honey
1/8 teaspoon salt
1/2 teaspoon grated orange rind
1/2 teaspoon Dijon mustard
4 cups torn Boston lettuce
1 1/2 cups (1-inch) cubed sourdough bread (about 3 ounces), toasted
1 cup shredded radicchio
1/3 cup chopped prosciutto (about 1 ounce)
1/2 cup orange sections

1. Bring 2 quarts water to a boil in a large saucepan. Cook haricots verts in boiling water 2 minutes or until crisp-tender. Drain and rinse with cold water; drain.
2. Combine oil and next 5 ingredients (through Dijon mustard) in a large bowl; stir well with a whisk. Add haricots verts, lettuce, and remaining ingredients to bowl; toss gently to coat. Yield: 6 servings (serving size: about 1⅓ cups).

CALORIES 105; **FAT** 3.2g (sat 0.5g, mono 0.6g, poly 1.6g); **PROTEIN** 4.4g; **CARB** 15.7g; **FIBER** 2.5g; **CHOL** 3mg; **IRON** 1.4mg; **SODIUM** 264mg; **CALC** 40mg

BALSAMIC VINEGAR

Made in Italy from trebbiano grapes, balsamic vinegar becomes sweeter and darker the longer it is aged. For rich flavor in salads, use older, higher-quality balsamic vinegar; it's a great counterpoint to bitter greens.

100-CALORIE
SALAD BOOSTERS

Start with 1½ cups of fresh mixed greens. Add a tablespoon of your favorite vinaigrette. Then pile on the good stuff. This tasty combo gives you crunch, sweetness, and piquant flavor.

1 TABLESPOON CRUMBLED BLUE CHEESE

+

1 TABLESPOON SWEETENED DRIED CRANBERRIES

+

1 TABLESPOON CHOPPED TOASTED WALNUTS

ROMAINE SALAD WITH BALSAMIC VINAIGRETTE

Customize this basic salad by using other fruit, such as dried cranberries, apricots, or raisins, or different cheeses, like blue or goat.

3 tablespoons balsamic vinegar
2 tablespoons olive oil
1 tablespoon minced shallots
1 tablespoon chopped fresh parsley
1 teaspoon Dijon mustard
1/8 teaspoon salt
1/4 teaspoon freshly ground black pepper
1 garlic clove, crushed
6 cups chopped romaine lettuce
1/4 cup dried cherries, chopped
2 tablespoons crumbled feta cheese

1. Combine first 8 ingredients in a large bowl; stir well with a whisk. Add lettuce, dried cherries, and cheese; toss gently to coat. Yield: 4 servings (serving size: 1½ cups).

CALORIES 131; **FAT** 8g (sat 1.7g, mono 5.2g, poly 0.9g); **PROTEIN** 2g; **CARB** 13.1g; **FIBER** 2.6g; **CHOL** 4mg; **IRON** 1.2mg; **SODIUM** 167mg; **CALC** 64mg

SUPERFAST / VEGETARIAN

ROMANO BEAN SALAD

Also called Italian flat beans or runner beans, this snap bean variety looks like a wide, flat green bean. You can easily substitute an equal amount of regular green beans.

2 quarts water
2/3 pound Romano beans, trimmed and cut into 1/2-inch pieces
2 teaspoons kosher salt
1 garlic clove
2 1/2 tablespoons chopped fresh flat-leaf parsley
4 teaspoons capers
2 teaspoons extra-virgin olive oil
3/4 teaspoon grated lemon rind
1/8 teaspoon kosher salt
1/8 teaspoon freshly ground black pepper

1. Bring 2 quarts water to a boil in a large saucepan. Add beans, 2 teaspoons salt, and garlic; cook 8 minutes or until tender. Drain and plunge beans into ice water; drain.
2. Place beans in a medium bowl. Finely chop garlic; add to beans. Add parsley and remaining ingredients, tossing gently to coat. Yield: 4 servings (serving size: ½ cup).

CALORIES 46; **FAT** 2.4g (sat 0.3g, mono 1.7g, poly 0.3g); **PROTEIN** 1.5g; **CARB** 6g; **FIBER** 2.8g; **CHOL** 0mg; **IRON** 1mg; **SODIUM** 247mg; **CALC** 34mg

VEGETARIAN

SUMMER'S BEST GARDEN SALAD

3 tablespoons fresh lime juice
2 teaspoons honey
1/2 teaspoon Dijon mustard
1/4 teaspoon salt
1/4 teaspoon freshly ground black pepper
2 teaspoons extra-virgin olive oil
4 cups shredded romaine lettuce
1 cup yellow pear tomatoes, halved
1 cup chopped peeled cucumber
1/2 cup finely chopped orange bell pepper
1/2 cup thinly sliced radishes
2 tablespoons chopped fresh chives
1 small yellow squash, halved lengthwise and thinly sliced (about 1 cup)
1/2 cup chopped avocado

1. Combine first 5 ingredients in a small bowl. Gradually add oil, stirring with a whisk.
2. Combine lettuce and next 6 ingredients (through squash) in a large bowl. Drizzle dressing over lettuce mixture, and toss gently to coat. Top with avocado. Yield: 6 servings (serving size: about 1 cup salad and 4 teaspoons avocado).

CALORIES 64; **FAT** 3.7g (sat 0.6g, mono 2.3g, poly 0.5g); **PROTEIN** 1.6g; **CARB** 7.8g; **FIBER** 2.4g; **CHOL** 0mg; **IRON** 0.9mg; **SODIUM** 123mg; **CALC** 28mg

SUPERFAST

SHAVED SUMMER SQUASH SALAD WITH PROSCIUTTO CRISPS

Summer squash is delicious raw when it's shaved and marinated with a bit of salt.

1 medium zucchini
2 medium yellow squash
¼ teaspoon salt
2 tablespoons thinly sliced fresh mint
1 tablespoon extra-virgin olive oil
½ teaspoon grated lemon rind
1 teaspoon fresh lemon juice
¼ teaspoon freshly ground black pepper
3 thin slices prosciutto (1 ounce), chopped
¼ cup (1 ounce) crumbled ricotta salata or feta cheese

1. Shave zucchini and squash into thin strips using a vegetable peeler. Discard seeds. Place zucchini and squash in a medium bowl, and toss with salt.
2. Combine mint and next 4 ingredients (through pepper) in a small bowl; stir with a whisk. Pour over zucchini and squash; toss.
3. Heat a small nonstick skillet over medium heat. Add prosciutto; sauté 2 minutes or until crisp.
4. Arrange ¾ cup salad on each of 4 plates. Top each serving with 1 tablespoon cheese; sprinkle evenly with prosciutto. Yield: 4 servings.

CALORIES 68; **FAT** 4.9g (sat 1.1g, mono 3g, poly 0.7g); **PROTEIN** 3.5g; **CARB** 3.6g; **FIBER** 1.1g; **CHOL** 6mg; **IRON** 0.5mg; **SODIUM** 269mg; **CALC** 36mg

RICOTTA SALATA

Ricotta salata is a crumbly, salty sheep's milk cheese. If you can't find it, pungent feta is just as tasty.

MAKE-AHEAD / PORTABLE / VEGETARIAN

SMOKED POTATO SALAD

Prepare this salad as a treat for an outdoor get-together.

2 cups mesquite wood chips
¼ cup olive oil, divided
½ teaspoon freshly ground black pepper
¼ teaspoon kosher salt
1½ pounds small potatoes
⅓ cup sliced pitted kalamata olives
2 thinly sliced green onions
2 tablespoons chopped fresh flat-leaf parsley
1 tablespoon red wine vinegar
2 teaspoons celery seed
1 teaspoon Dijon mustard

1. Soak wood chips in water 1 hour; drain.
2. Remove grill rack, and set aside. Prepare grill for indirect grilling, heating one side to medium-high and leaving one side with no heat. Maintain temperature at 400°. Pierce bottom of a disposable foil pan several times with the tip of a knife. Place pan on heat element on heated side of grill; add 1 cup wood chips to pan. Place grill rack on grill. Combine 1 tablespoon oil, pepper, salt, and potatoes in a medium bowl; toss to coat. Arrange potatoes in a single layer in a disposable foil pan. Place pan over unheated side; close lid. Cook 30 minutes at 400° or until tender, adding remaining 1 cup wood chips after 15 minutes. Remove potatoes from grill. Combine potatoes, olives, and onions in a medium bowl.
3. Combine 3 tablespoons oil, parsley, and next 3 ingredients (through mustard) in a small bowl; stir with a whisk. Drizzle vinaigrette over potato mixture; toss well. Yield: 8 servings (serving size: about ¾ cup).

CALORIES 162; **FAT** 8.8g (sat 1.2g, mono 6.4g, poly 1g); **PROTEIN** 2.4g; **CARB** 19.4g; **FIBER** 2.2g; **CHOL** 0mg; **IRON** 1.4mg; **SODIUM** 194mg; **CALC** 29mg

SUPERFAST / VEGETARIAN

SPINACH, ENDIVE, AND TANGELO SALAD

This salad hits a lot of flavorful notes: sweet fruit, earthy nuts, refreshing mint, and slight bitterness from Belgian endive. Though you can buy Belgian endive year-round, it peaks between November and April. Choose tightly packed heads with lightly colored tips.

2 tablespoons torn mint leaves
1½ teaspoons grated tangelo rind
1 tablespoon fresh tangelo juice
2 teaspoons thinly sliced green onions
½ teaspoon champagne or white wine vinegar
¼ teaspoon salt
2 tablespoons walnut oil
4 cups baby spinach leaves
¾ cup sliced peeled tangelo
2 heads Belgian endive, halved and thinly sliced
⅓ cup walnuts, toasted
¼ teaspoon freshly ground black pepper

1. Combine first 6 ingredients in a medium bowl. Gradually add walnut oil, stirring constantly with a whisk.
2. Combine spinach, tangelo slices, and endive in a large bowl. Drizzle dressing over salad, tossing to coat. Arrange 1 cup salad on each of 6 plates, and sprinkle evenly with walnuts and black pepper. Serve immediately. Yield: 6 servings.

CALORIES 119; **FAT** 9.1g (sat 0.8g, mono 1.6g, poly 6g); **PROTEIN** 2.3g; **CARB** 10.6g; **FIBER** 3.3g; **CHOL** 0mg; **IRON** 0.9mg; **SODIUM** 115mg; **CALC** 54mg

TANGELOS

Tangelos, a cross between mandarin oranges and grapefruit or pomelo, have a small neck at the top of the fruit. Find them as early as October.

SUPERFAST / VEGETARIAN

SPINACH SALAD WITH GORGONZOLA, PISTACHIOS, AND PEPPER JELLY VINAIGRETTE

Red pepper jelly adds the snappy note to the vinaigrette that makes this salad memorable. If time is tight around dinnertime, prepare the vinaigrette (Step 1) earlier in the day and refrigerate it; let it come to room temperature before tossing it with the spinach.

1/4 cup red pepper jelly
2 tablespoons cider vinegar
1 tablespoon extra-virgin olive oil
1/8 teaspoon kosher salt
1/8 teaspoon freshly ground black pepper
8 cups fresh baby spinach
1/4 cup (1 ounce) crumbled Gorgonzola cheese
1/4 cup dry-roasted pistachios

1. Place jelly in a 1-cup glass measure. Microwave at HIGH 30 seconds. Add cider vinegar, oil, salt, and black pepper, stirring with a whisk until blended. Cool to room temperature.
2. Combine spinach and cheese in a large bowl. Drizzle vinaigrette over spinach mixture; toss well. Sprinkle with nuts. Serve immediately. Yield: 6 servings (serving size: 1 cup spinach mixture and 2 teaspoons nuts).

CALORIES 101; **FAT** 6.1g (sat 1.6g, mono 3g, poly 1.1g); **PROTEIN** 2.9g; **CARB** 10.4g; **FIBER** 2.3g; **CHOL** 4mg; **IRON** 1.3mg; **SODIUM** 187mg; **CALC** 54mg

GORGONZOLA

A cow's milk cheese from Italy, Gorgonzola has bluish-green veins and is aged at least three months. If you prefer a milder flavor, look for Gorgonzola dolce, which is younger.

KID-FRIENDLY / SUPERFAST / VEGETARIAN

SPINACH-STRAWBERRY SALAD

Use organic, locally grown strawberries in spring when you can find them. Their intensely sweet flavor, combined with the mint and vinaigrette, makes this salad sublime.

1½ cups quartered strawberries
¼ cup Easy Herb Vinaigrette (page 13)
1 tablespoon finely chopped fresh mint
1 (6-ounce) package fresh baby spinach
2 tablespoons sliced almonds, toasted
¼ teaspoon freshly ground black pepper

1. Combine strawberries, ¼ cup Easy Herb Vinaigrette, mint, and spinach in a large bowl; toss gently to coat. Sprinkle with almonds and pepper; serve immediately. Yield: 4 servings (serving size: 2 cups).

CALORIES 136; **FAT** 10.3g (sat 0.7g, mono 6g, poly 3g); **PROTEIN** 2.1g; **CARB** 11g; **FIBER** 3.6g; **CHOL** 0mg; **IRON** 1.7mg; **SODIUM** 113mg; **CALC** 50mg

LEMONS

The tartness of lemons can vary, so always taste a lemon-based dressing on a lettuce leaf, and adjust the dressing to your liking.

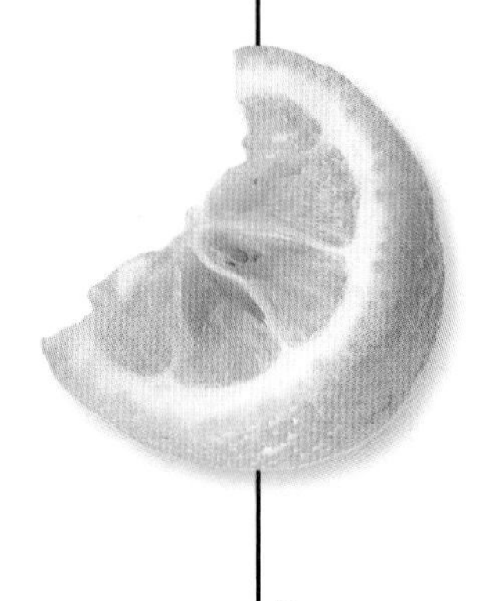

SUPERFAST / VEGETARIAN

TOMATO, CUCUMBER, AND FENNEL SALAD

1½ tablespoons lemon juice
1 tablespoon olive oil
⅛ teaspoon salt
⅛ teaspoon freshly ground black pepper
2 cups sliced cucumber
½ cup quartered cherry tomatoes
¼ cup sliced fennel bulb

1. Combine lemon juice, olive oil, salt, and pepper in a small bowl.
2. Combine cucumber, cherry tomatoes, and sliced fennel bulb in a medium bowl. Pour dressing over vegetables; toss. Yield: 4 servings (serving size: about ⅔ cup).

CALORIES 44; **FAT** 3.6g (sat 0.5g, mono 2.5g, poly 0.5g); **PROTEIN** 0.6g; **CARB** 3.5g; **FIBER** 0.7g; **CHOL** 0mg; **IRON** 0.3mg; **SODIUM** 79mg; **CALC** 14mg

MAKE-AHEAD / PORTABLE

WARM POTATO SALAD WITH RAMPS AND BACON

Ramps and new potatoes, a wonderful, edible ode to spring, pair well together. If you've missed ramp season or you can't find them, substitute thin leeks.

1½ pounds new potatoes
3 tablespoons water
3 tablespoons extra-virgin olive oil
2 tablespoons white wine vinegar
1½ tablespoons Dijon mustard
2 bacon slices, cut into ½-inch pieces
10 ramps
1 cup thinly sliced radishes (about 8 radishes)
¼ teaspoon salt
¼ teaspoon freshly ground black pepper

1. Preheat oven to 375°.
2. Place potatoes in a 13 x 9–inch glass or ceramic baking dish, and drizzle with 3 tablespoons water. Cover with foil, and bake at 375° for 45 minutes or until tender. Remove foil, and cool 15 minutes. Halve potatoes.
3. Combine olive oil, vinegar, and mustard in a small bowl, stirring with a whisk. Cook bacon in a large nonstick skillet over medium heat until crisp, stirring occasionally. Remove bacon from pan using a slotted spoon, reserving drippings in pan. Increase heat to medium-high. Place potatoes, cut sides down, in pan; cook 5 minutes or until golden brown. Place potatoes in a medium bowl.
4. Remove and discard roots and outer leaves from ramps; rinse and drain ramps. Pat ramps dry. Thinly slice bulb ends and leaves crosswise to measure ½ cup. Add ramps, bacon, and radishes to potatoes. Drizzle dressing over potato mixture, and sprinkle with salt and pepper. Toss. Yield: 6 servings (serving size: ⅔ cup).

CALORIES 170; **FAT** 8.7g (sat 1.6g, mono 5g, poly 1.1g); **PROTEIN** 3.8g; **CARB** 21.2g; **FIBER** 2.8g; **CHOL** 3mg; **IRON** 1.3mg; **SODIUM** 223mg; **CALC** 33mg

RAMPS

Meet the elusive ramp: a beautifully wispy distant cousin to the onion. Also called wild leeks, ramps are available for only about six weeks in spring, and you can usually find them in farmers' markets. Don't be deceived by their delicate, lilylike leaves: These alliums pack a pungent, garlicky bite balanced by a faint whiff of musk. Edible from end to end, a few go a long way.

VEGETARIAN

WINTER SALAD WITH ROASTED BEETS AND CITRUS REDUCTION DRESSING

Using fresh orange juice, multicolored beets, and—for good measure—some creamy, tangy goat cheese, this starter salad celebrates the produce of the season and makes a knockout-gorgeous addition to the table.

4 medium beets (red and golden)
Cooking spray
3/4 cup fresh orange juice (about 4 oranges)
1/2 teaspoon sugar
1 tablespoon minced shallots
2 tablespoons white wine vinegar
3/4 teaspoon kosher salt, divided
1/2 teaspoon freshly ground black pepper, divided
1/4 cup extra-virgin olive oil
4 cups torn Boston lettuce
2 cups trimmed watercress
2 cups torn radicchio
1/2 cup (2 ounces) crumbled goat cheese

1. Preheat oven to 400°.
2. Leave root and 1-inch stem on beets; scrub with a brush. Place beets on a foil-lined jelly-roll pan coated with cooking spray. Lightly coat beets with cooking spray. Bake at 400° for 1 hour and 10 minutes or until tender. Cool beets slightly. Trim off beet roots and stems; rub off skins. Cut beets into ½-inch-thick wedges.
3. Bring juice and sugar to a boil in a small saucepan; cook 10 minutes or until reduced to 2 tablespoons. Pour into a medium bowl; cool slightly. Add shallots, vinegar, ½ teaspoon salt, and ¼ teaspoon pepper, stirring with a whisk. Gradually add oil, stirring constantly with a whisk.
4. Combine lettuce, watercress, and radicchio in a large bowl. Sprinkle lettuce mixture with ¼ teaspoon salt and ¼ teaspoon pepper; toss gently to combine. Arrange about 1 cup lettuce mixture on each of 8 plates. Divide beets evenly among salads. Drizzle about 1 tablespoon dressing over each salad; sprinkle each salad with 1 tablespoon cheese. Yield: 8 servings.

CALORIES 127; **FAT** 9.1g (sat 2.4g, mono 5.4g, poly 0.8g); **PROTEIN** 3.1g; **CARB** 8.2g; **FIBER** 1.7g; **CHOL** 6mg; **IRON** 1mg; **SODIUM** 253mg; **CALC** 53mg

PEPPER

A pepper mill is a good investment: You'll get the best flavor out of peppercorns if you grind them over a salad right before serving. Buy whole dried black peppercorns, and store them in a cool, dark place at room temperature; they will last up to a year.

MAKE-AHEAD / VEGETARIAN

YELLOW PLUM SALAD

As gorgeous as it is delicious, this salad will become a summer staple. Serve it with grilled chicken, pork, steaks, or seafood. Look for Mirabelle or other golden-fleshed plums.

2 yellow bell peppers
4 golden beets (about 12 ounces)
2½ tablespoons extra-virgin olive oil
1 tablespoon white wine vinegar
1 tablespoon chopped fresh chives
1 teaspoon chopped fresh thyme
1 teaspoon Dijon mustard
¼ teaspoon salt
⅛ teaspoon freshly ground black pepper
8 yellow-fleshed plums, halved and pitted (about 1 pound)
1 cup yellow pear tomatoes, halved lengthwise
½ cup (2 ounces) crumbled goat cheese

1. Preheat broiler to high.
2. Cut bell peppers in half lengthwise; discard seeds and membranes. Place pepper halves, skin sides up, on a foil-lined baking sheet; flatten with hand. Broil 13 minutes or until blackened. Place in a paper bag, and fold tightly to seal. Let stand 20 minutes. Peel and cut bell peppers into ½-inch-thick strips.
3. Preheat oven to 450°.
4. Leave root and 1-inch stem on beets; scrub with a brush. Place beets in an 11 x 7–inch glass or ceramic baking dish. Add 1 inch of water to dish; cover tightly with foil. Bake at 450° for 1 hour or until tender. Cool; peel and cut into ½-inch-thick slices.
5. Combine olive oil and next 6 ingredients (through black pepper) in a small bowl, stirring well with a whisk. Place sliced beets in a medium bowl. Drizzle beets with 3 tablespoons vinaigrette; toss gently. Let stand at least 15 minutes. Divide beets evenly among 6 plates, and top each evenly with peppers, plums, and tomatoes. Drizzle each serving with remaining vinaigrette. Sprinkle evenly with cheese. Yield: 6 servings.

CALORIES 158; **FAT** 8g (sat 2.2g, mono 4.6g, poly 0.7g); **PROTEIN** 4.2g; **CARB** 20.2g; **FIBER** 3.5g; **CHOL** 4mg; **IRON** 1.4mg; **SODIUM** 194mg; **CALC** 35mg

WINTER JEWELED FRUIT SALAD

In Mexico, copas de frutas *(fruit cups) are popular street food. They typically consist of fresh fruit sprinkled with lime juice and chili powder, and are the inspiration for this jewel-colored fruit salad. Jicama (pronounced HEE-kah-mah), also known as a Mexican potato or turnip, tastes like a cross between an apple and a potato, and adds crunch to the salad.*

1/2 cup pomegranate seeds (about 1 pomegranate)
1/2 cup julienne-cut peeled jicama
1/3 cup sliced seeded kumquats (about 6 medium)
2 medium ripe mangoes, peeled and cut into thin slices
2 tangerines or clementines, peeled and sectioned
2 blood oranges, peeled and sectioned
1 pear, thinly sliced
2 tablespoons fresh lime juice
2 tablespoons honey
1/4 teaspoon ground red pepper
1/8 teaspoon coarse sea salt

1. Combine first 7 ingredients in a large bowl; toss gently.
2. Combine lime juice and next 3 ingredients (through salt) in a small bowl, stirring well with a whisk. Pour over fruit; toss gently to coat. Serve at room temperature. Yield: 8 servings (serving size: 1 cup).

CALORIES 118; **FAT** 0.4g (sat 0.1g, mono 0.1g, poly 0.1g); **PROTEIN** 1.3g; **CARB** 30g; **FIBER** 4.2g; **CHOL** 0mg; **IRON** 0.4mg; **SODIUM** 37mg; **CALC** 39mg

POMEGRANATES

One of the oldest cultivated fruits in the world, pomegranates are available only from September through January. Look for fruit that is round, plump, and blemish-free. The bigger the fruit, the better, as they tend to be juiciest.

pasta, breads, beans & grains

Chewy, toothsome starches add texture, substance, and even an element of comfort to salads. Best of all, they're ideal for carrying lots of flavor in every bite.

CONFETTI COUSCOUS, p. 106 →

MAKE-AHEAD / PORTABLE

CONFETTI COUSCOUS

Serve this salad chilled or at room temperature. You can prepare the recipe up to a day ahead, but stir in the basil just before serving.

2 baby eggplants, cut into ½-inch-thick slices
2 yellow squash, cut into ½-inch-thick slices
2 red bell peppers, seeded and cut into quarters
⅓ cup extra-virgin olive oil, divided
1 teaspoon salt, divided
½ teaspoon freshly ground black pepper, divided
2 cups water
1½ cups fat-free, lower-sodium chicken broth
2 cups uncooked Israeli couscous
3 tablespoons red wine vinegar
1½ tablespoons Dijon mustard
½ cup chopped fresh basil

1. Preheat grill to medium-high heat.
2. Brush eggplants, squash, and bell peppers evenly with 4 teaspoons oil. Sprinkle evenly with ¼ teaspoon salt and ¼ teaspoon black pepper. Place vegetables on grill rack; grill 3 minutes on each side or until slightly charred. Cool and chop. Place vegetables in a large bowl.
3. Bring 2 cups water and broth to a boil in a medium saucepan. Stir in couscous. Reduce heat, and simmer 8 minutes or until couscous is tender. Drain and rinse with cold water. Add couscous, ¾ teaspoon salt, and ¼ teaspoon pepper to vegetable mixture; toss. Combine vinegar and mustard in a medium bowl, stirring well. Gradually add ¼ cup oil to vinegar mixture, stirring constantly with a whisk. Drizzle vinegar mixture over couscous mixture; toss to coat. Stir in basil. Yield: 8 servings (serving size: 1 cup).

CALORIES 271; **FAT** 9.8g (sat 1.4g, mono 6.7g, poly 1.5g); **PROTEIN** 6.8g; **CARB** 39.3g; **FIBER** 4.6g; **CHOL** 0mg; **IRON** 1mg; **SODIUM** 453mg; **CALC** 29mg

MAKE-AHEAD / PORTABLE / SUPERFAST / VEGETARIAN

ORZO SALAD WITH RADISH AND FENNEL ➤

Lemony dressing and fresh mint add vibrant flavor to this pasta salad. Serve chilled or at room temperature, and garnish with pretty mint leaves, if desired.

8 ounces uncooked orzo (rice-shaped pasta)
1 tablespoon kosher salt
¼ cup fresh lemon juice
3 tablespoons olive oil
1 teaspoon Dijon mustard
½ teaspoon freshly ground black pepper
1½ cups diced fennel (about 1 bulb)
½ cup chopped radishes
3 tablespoons chopped fresh mint
3 tablespoons minced green onions
½ teaspoon kosher salt
⅓ cup pine nuts, toasted
Mint sprigs (optional)

1. Cook pasta with 1 tablespoon kosher salt according to package directions, omitting additional fat. Drain and rinse with cold water. Drain well.
2. Combine lemon juice and next 3 ingredients (through pepper) in a large bowl; stir well with a whisk. Add pasta, fennel, and next 4 ingredients (through ½ teaspoon salt); toss well to coat. Cover and chill. Top with nuts and mint, if desired, before serving. Yield: 4 servings (serving size: 1¼ cups salad and 4 teaspoons nuts).

CALORIES 393; **FAT** 19.1g (sat 2.3g, mono 9.6g, poly 5.4g); **PROTEIN** 10g; **CARB** 48.8g; **FIBER** 4.1g; **CHOL** 0mg; **IRON** 3.3mg; **SODIUM** 517mg; **CALC** 46mg

THE GUIDE TO

PASTA

For salads, use noodles when you have thick, smooth dressings to coat them, such as a peanut sauce. Use short and tubular pastas in salads with chunky ingredients. They are good companions with diced vegetables, beans, or meats. Shapes to try:

WHOLE-GRAIN PASTAS TO TRY: The newest whole-grain pastas boast far better taste than the versions of the '70s and '80s, thanks in part to improved technology that creates a smoother, less grainy texture. Try brown rice penne in salads, or branch out to pastas made with less familiar grains like spelt and kamut. Remember that whole-grain pastas tend to soak up more sauce than refined-flour pastas, so serve your salads immediately after you dress them, or consider packing the dressing in a separate container if you're taking your salad to go.

MAKE-AHEAD / PORTABLE / SUPERFAST / VEGETARIAN

COUSCOUS SALAD WITH CHICKPEAS

1 cup uncooked whole-wheat couscous
1/2 teaspoon salt, divided
1/2 teaspoon freshly ground black pepper, divided
1/8 teaspoon ground cinnamon
1 cup boiling water
3 tablespoons extra-virgin olive oil
3 tablespoons fresh lemon juice
1 1/2 teaspoons minced garlic
Dash of sugar
1/3 cup torn mint leaves
1/4 cup thinly sliced green onions
1/8 teaspoon smoked paprika
1 (15-ounce) can chickpeas (garbanzo beans), rinsed and drained
1 1/2 cups halved cherry tomatoes
3/4 cup (3 ounces) crumbled feta cheese

1. Place couscous, ¼ teaspoon salt, ¼ teaspoon pepper, and cinnamon in a bowl. Stir in 1 cup boiling water; cover and let stand 10 minutes. Fluff with a fork.
2. Combine oil, juice, garlic, and sugar.
3. Add oil mixture, ¼ teaspoon salt, ¼ teaspoon pepper, mint, and next 4 ingredients (through tomatoes) to couscous. Sprinkle with cheese. Yield: 4 servings (serving size: 1⅓ cups salad and 3 tablespoons cheese).

CALORIES 351; **FAT** 16.2g (sat 4.7g, mono 8.6g, poly 1.6g); **PROTEIN** 11g; **CARB** 43.6g; **FIBER** 7.7g; **CHOL** 19mg; **IRON** 2.6mg; **SODIUM** 655mg; **CALC** 154mg

COUSCOUS

Made from semolina flour (a product of durum wheat), quick-cooking couscous is fine for salads; after cooking, fluff with a fork to separate the grains before mixing it with a dressing and other ingredients.

MAKE-AHEAD / VEGETARIAN

FETA AND GREEN ONION COUSCOUS CAKES WITH TOMATO-OLIVE SALAD

Couscous cakes serve as an excellent base for fresh tomatoes and parsley. You can make the cakes a day ahead; finish the salad right before serving.

Cakes:

1/3 cup uncooked whole-wheat couscous
1/2 cup boiling water
1/4 cup (1 ounce) crumbled feta cheese
3 tablespoons egg substitute
2 tablespoons finely chopped green onions
1/8 teaspoon freshly ground black pepper
Cooking spray
2 teaspoons olive oil

Salad:

2/3 cup chopped seeded tomato
2 tablespoons chopped pitted kalamata olives
2 tablespoons chopped fresh parsley
2 teaspoons red wine vinegar
1/2 teaspoon olive oil
1/8 teaspoon freshly ground black pepper
3 cups gourmet salad greens

1. To prepare cakes, place couscous in a medium bowl; stir in ½ cup boiling water. Cover and let stand 5 minutes or until liquid is absorbed. Fluff with a fork. Cool slightly. Add cheese and next 3 ingredients (through pepper). Heat a large nonstick skillet over medium-high heat. Coat pan with cooking spray. Add 2 teaspoons oil to pan; swirl to coat. Spoon about ⅓ cup couscous mixture into 4 mounds in pan. Lightly press with a spatula to flatten to ½ inch. Cook 2 minutes or until lightly browned. Coat tops of cakes with cooking spray. Carefully turn cakes over; cook 2 minutes or until heated.
2. To prepare salad, combine tomato and next 5 ingredients (through ⅛ teaspoon pepper). Arrange 1½ cups greens on each of 2 plates. Arrange 2 cakes over each serving; top each serving with ½ cup tomato mixture. Yield: 2 servings.

CALORIES 289; **FAT** 14g (sat 3.6g, mono 8.1g, poly 1.8g); **PROTEIN** 10.7g; **CARB** 30.6g; **FIBER** 4.4g; **CHOL** 13mg; **IRON** 2.7mg; **SODIUM** 478mg; **CALC** 154mg

MAKE-AHEAD / VEGETARIAN

GEMELLI SALAD WITH GREEN BEANS, PISTACHIOS, AND LEMON-THYME VINAIGRETTE

If you can't find haricots verts, use trimmed regular green beans, but add them to the pasta after eight minutes of cooking since they'll take longer to cook. You can make the salad ahead; dress it just before serving so the beans don't turn drab.

8 ounces uncooked gemelli (short twisted tube pasta)
1 cup (1½-inch) cut haricots verts (about 4 ounces)
½ cup chopped shelled pistachios
2 tablespoons fresh thyme leaves, divided
2 tablespoons grated lemon rind, divided
1 tablespoon minced shallots
2 tablespoons champagne or white wine vinegar
3 garlic cloves, crushed
5 tablespoons extra-virgin olive oil
¼ teaspoon kosher salt
½ teaspoon freshly ground black pepper
1 ounce shaved fresh Parmesan cheese (about ⅓ cup)

1. Cook pasta according to package directions, omitting salt and fat. Add haricots verts during final 2 minutes of cooking. Drain and rinse pasta mixture under cold water; drain well.

2. Place pasta mixture, pistachios, 1 tablespoon thyme, and 1 tablespoon lemon rind in a large bowl; toss gently to combine.

3. Combine 1 tablespoon thyme, 1 tablespoon lemon rind, shallots, vinegar, and garlic in a small bowl, stirring well with a whisk. Gradually add olive oil, stirring constantly with a whisk. Add salt and black pepper; stir with a whisk. Drizzle over pasta mixture, and toss gently to coat. Top each serving with Parmesan cheese. Yield: 5 servings (serving size: about 1 cup salad and about 1 tablespoon cheese).

CALORIES 395; **FAT** 22g (sat 3.9g, mono 13.4g, poly 3.8g); **PROTEIN** 11.6g; **CARB** 41.3g; **FIBER** 3.8g; **CHOL** 5mg; **IRON** 2.5mg; **SODIUM** 188mg; **CALC** 105mg

HARICOTS VERTS

Picked young and prized for their intense, slightly sweet flavor and crisp texture, these tiny beans are also referred to as French filet beans. Choose beans that are no longer than about three inches and only a bit larger in diameter than a matchstick.

KID-FRIENDLY

MACARONI SALAD WITH BACON, PEAS, AND CREAMY DIJON DRESSING

The tangy dressing contrasts well with the smoky bacon, sweet bell pepper, and pungent red onion.

Dressing:

1/2 cup (4 ounces) 1/3-less-fat cream cheese
1/4 cup chopped shallots
1/4 cup reduced-fat mayonnaise
2 tablespoons fat-free sour cream
2 tablespoons Dijon mustard
2 tablespoons fresh lemon juice
1 tablespoon white wine vinegar
3/4 teaspoon freshly ground black pepper
1/2 teaspoon kosher salt

Salad:

8 ounces uncooked large elbow macaroni
2/3 cup fresh green peas
2/3 cup finely diced red bell pepper
2/3 cup finely diced red onion
1/2 cup thinly sliced green onions
1/4 cup chopped fresh flat-leaf parsley
1/2 teaspoon grated lemon rind
3 lower-sodium bacon slices, cooked and crumbled

1. To prepare dressing, place first 9 ingredients in a food processor, and process until smooth. Cover and chill.
2. To prepare salad, cook pasta according to package directions, omitting salt and fat; add peas during last 3 minutes of cooking time. Drain; rinse with cold water. Drain. Combine pasta mixture, bell pepper, and next 4 ingredients (through rind) in a large bowl. Toss pasta mixture with half of dressing. Cover and chill until ready to serve. Toss salad with remaining dressing, and sprinkle with crumbled bacon; serve immediately. Yield: 8 servings (serving size: 1 cup salad and about 1 teaspoon bacon).

CALORIES 208; **FAT** 7g (sat 3.2g, mono 2.2g, poly 1.4g); **PROTEIN** 8.6g; **CARB** 29.1g; **FIBER** 2.3g; **CHOL** 16mg; **IRON** 1.5mg; **SODIUM** 454mg; **CALC** 44mg

KID-FRIENDLY / MAKE-AHEAD / PORTABLE / SUPERFAST

LEMONY ORZO-VEGGIE SALAD WITH CHICKEN

Pack for lunch with some crunchy crackers.

3/4 cup uncooked orzo
1/4 teaspoon grated lemon rind
3 tablespoons fresh lemon juice
1 tablespoon extra-virgin olive oil
1/2 teaspoon kosher salt
1/2 teaspoon minced garlic
1/4 teaspoon honey
1/8 teaspoon freshly ground black pepper
1 cup shredded skinless, boneless rotisserie chicken breast
1/2 cup diced English cucumber
1/2 cup prechopped red bell pepper
1/3 cup thinly sliced green onions
1 tablespoon chopped fresh dill
1/2 cup (2 ounces) crumbled goat cheese

1. Cook orzo according to package directions, omitting salt and fat. Drain and rinse with cold water; drain and place in a large bowl.
2. While orzo cooks, combine lemon rind and next 6 ingredients (through black pepper), stirring well with a whisk. Drizzle juice mixture over orzo; toss to coat. Add chicken and next 4 ingredients (through dill); toss gently to combine. Sprinkle with cheese. Yield: 4 servings (serving size: about 1¼ cups).

CALORIES 275; **FAT** 9.7g (sat 3.8g, mono 3.9g, poly 0.9g); **PROTEIN** 18.2g; **CARB** 28g; **FIBER** 1.8g; **CHOL** 41mg; **IRON** 0.9mg; **SODIUM** 338mg; **CALC** 60mg

MAKE-AHEAD / PORTABLE / VEGETARIAN

ORZO SALAD WITH SPICY BUTTERMILK DRESSING

Buttermilk and sour cream combine to give this pasta salad a tangy flavor. You can make this salad ahead through Step 2; store the dressing in the refrigerator, and when you're ready to serve, top with the dressing, avocado, and parsley.

1 cup uncooked orzo
1 cup frozen whole-kernel corn, thawed and drained
12 cherry tomatoes, quartered
3 green onions, sliced
1 (15-ounce) can black beans, rinsed and drained
1/4 cup low-fat buttermilk (1%)
3 tablespoons chopped fresh cilantro, divided
3 tablespoons fresh lime juice
2 tablespoons light sour cream
2 tablespoons canola mayonnaise
1 teaspoon chili powder
1/2 teaspoon kosher salt
1/4 teaspoon freshly ground black pepper
1/4 teaspoon ground red pepper
2 garlic cloves, crushed
1 peeled avocado, cut into 8 wedges
1 tablespoon chopped fresh parsley

1. Cook orzo according to package directions, omitting salt and fat. Drain and rinse; drain well. Place orzo, corn, and next 3 ingredients (through beans) in a large bowl; toss.
2. Combine buttermilk, 2 tablespoons cilantro, and next 8 ingredients (through garlic) in a small bowl, stirring well with a whisk.
3. Drizzle buttermilk dressing over orzo mixture; toss. Top with avocado; garnish with remaining cilantro and parsley. Yield: 4 servings (serving size: 1¾ cups salad, 2 avocado wedges, ¾ teaspoon cilantro, and ¾ teaspoon parsley).

CALORIES 424; **FAT** 15.3g (sat 2.3g, mono 8.4g, poly 2.7g); **PROTEIN** 12.7g; **CARB** 63.8g; **FIBER** 10.1g; **CHOL** 6mg; **IRON** 1.8mg; **SODIUM** 607mg; **CALC** 80mg

KID-FRIENDLY

PROSCIUTTO AND MELON PASTA SALAD

Substitute whole-wheat pasta, if you like.

8 ounces uncooked legume-based farfalle pasta
1½ tablespoons fresh lemon juice
1½ tablespoons white wine vinegar
¼ teaspoon Dijon mustard
¼ teaspoon salt
¼ teaspoon freshly ground black pepper
⅛ teaspoon ground red pepper
1 garlic clove, coarsely chopped
2½ tablespoons extra-virgin olive oil
1 cup baby arugula
¾ cup diced cantaloupe
¼ cup thinly vertically sliced shallots
2 tablespoons torn mint leaves
2 ounces thinly sliced prosciutto, cut into 2-inch-long strips
1 ounce shaved fresh Parmigiano-Reggiano cheese (about ⅓ cup)

1. Cook pasta according to package directions, omitting salt and fat. Drain; cool to room temperature.
2. Place lemon juice and next 6 ingredients (through garlic) in a food processor; process until blended. With processor on, slowly pour olive oil through food chute; process 15 seconds or until blended.
3. Combine cooled pasta, arugula, and next 4 ingredients (through prosciutto) in a large bowl. Drizzle dressing over salad just before serving, and toss gently to coat. Top salad with cheese. Yield: 4 servings (serving size: 1¼ cups).

CALORIES 357; **FAT** 12.8g (sat 2.9g, mono 7.5g, poly 1.6g); **PROTEIN** 16.8g; **CARB** 44.3g; **FIBER** 4.7g; **CHOL** 13mg; **IRON** 2.5mg; **SODIUM** 518mg; **CALC** 134mg

MAKE-AHEAD / PORTABLE

PEPPERY MONTEREY JACK PASTA SALAD

Acini di pepe [ah-CHEE-nee dee-PAY-pay] are tiny pasta rounds resembling peppercorns. Use ditalini (very short tube-shaped macaroni) or any other small pasta shape if you can't find acini di pepe in your supermarket. Serve with breadsticks.

6 ounces uncooked acini di pepe pasta
2¼ cups diced plum tomato (about 14 ounces)
¼ cup capers, rinsed and drained
¼ cup finely chopped red onion
¼ cup sliced pickled banana peppers
¼ cup chopped fresh parsley
2 tablespoons cider vinegar
1 tablespoon extra-virgin olive oil
½ teaspoon dried oregano
⅛ teaspoon salt
2 ounces Monterey Jack cheese, cut into ¼-inch cubes
1 (16-ounce) can navy beans, rinsed and drained
1 ounce salami, chopped
1 garlic clove, minced

1. Cook pasta according to package directions, omitting salt and fat. Drain.
2. Combine tomato and next 12 ingredients (through garlic) in a large bowl. Add pasta to tomato mixture, tossing well to combine. Yield: 12 servings (serving size: about ½ cup).

CALORIES 137; **FAT** 3.8g (sat 1.4g, mono 1.6g, poly 0.4g); **PROTEIN** 6.7g; **CARB** 19.8g; **FIBER** 2.9g; **CHOL** 7mg; **IRON** 1.4mg; **SODIUM** 252mg; **CALC** 62mg

VEGETARIAN

ROASTED ASPARAGUS AND TOMATO PENNE SALAD WITH GOAT CHEESE

Serve immediately, or cover and chill for two hours for a cold pasta salad.

2 cups uncooked penne or mostaccioli (tube-shaped pasta)
12 asparagus spears
12 cherry tomatoes
4 tablespoons extra-virgin olive oil, divided
3/8 teaspoon kosher salt, divided
1/2 teaspoon freshly ground black pepper, divided
1 tablespoon minced shallots
2 tablespoons fresh lemon juice
1 tablespoon Dijon mustard
1 teaspoon dried herbes de Provence
1 1/2 teaspoons honey
1/2 cup pitted kalamata olives, halved
2 cups baby arugula
1/2 cup (2 ounces) crumbled goat cheese

1. Preheat oven to 400°.
2. Cook pasta according to package directions, omitting salt and fat; drain and set aside.
3. Place asparagus and tomatoes on a jelly-roll pan. Drizzle with 1 tablespoon olive oil; sprinkle with ¼ teaspoon salt and ¼ teaspoon black pepper. Toss gently to coat; arrange asparagus and tomato mixture in a single layer. Bake at 400° for 6 minutes or until asparagus is crisp-tender. Remove asparagus from pan. Place pan back in oven, and bake tomatoes an additional 4 minutes. Remove tomatoes from pan; let asparagus and tomatoes stand 10 minutes. Cut asparagus into 1-inch lengths; cut tomatoes in half.
4. Combine shallots and next 4 ingredients (through honey) in a small bowl, stirring with a whisk. Gradually add 3 tablespoons oil, stirring constantly with a whisk. Stir in ⅛ teaspoon salt and ¼ teaspoon black pepper.
5. Place pasta, asparagus, tomato, olives, and arugula in a large bowl; toss. Drizzle dressing over pasta mixture; toss. Sprinkle with cheese.
Yield: 4 servings (serving size: about 1¼ cups salad and 2 tablespoons cheese).

CALORIES 408; **FAT** 22.3g (sat 5.5g, mono 13.7g, poly 2.1g); **PROTEIN** 11.3g; **CARB** 42.9g; **FIBER** 3.5g; **CHOL** 11mg; **IRON** 3.6mg; **SODIUM** 584mg; **CALC** 101mg

MAKE-AHEAD / PORTABLE

SOBA NOODLES WITH CHICKEN AND VEGETABLES

Serve this with a fruit salad of pineapple, mango, and kiwifruit. If you prefer a vegetable side dish, steamed sugar snap peas or snow peas are a great choice.

½ cup fat-free, lower-sodium chicken broth
3 tablespoons lower-sodium soy sauce
2 tablespoons oyster sauce
2 tablespoons mirin (sweet rice wine)
1 teaspoon Sriracha (hot chile sauce)
1 (12-ounce) package soba (buckwheat noodles)
1 tablespoon canola oil
1 teaspoon minced garlic
1 teaspoon grated peeled fresh ginger
1 pound chicken breast tenders, cut into bite-sized pieces
2 large zucchini, cut into julienne strips (about 2 cups)
1 large carrot, cut into julienne strips
1 tablespoon sesame seeds, toasted

1. Combine first 5 ingredients in a small bowl.
2. Prepare noodles according to package directions, omitting salt and fat. Drain and rinse with cold water; drain.
3. Heat a large nonstick skillet over medium-high heat. Add oil to pan; swirl to coat. Add garlic, ginger, and chicken to pan; sauté 3 minutes, stirring constantly. Add broth mixture, zucchini, and carrot to pan; cook 3 minutes, stirring constantly. Add noodles; cook 2 minutes or until thoroughly heated, tossing well. Sprinkle with sesame seeds. Yield: 6 servings (serving size: 1⅓ cups salad and ½ teaspoon seeds).

CALORIES 353; **FAT** 5.2g (sat 0.8g, mono 2.2g, poly 1.6g); **PROTEIN** 25.7g; **CARB** 47.4g; **FIBER** 2.4g; **CHOL** 44mg; **IRON** 4mg; **SODIUM** 754mg; **CALC** 29mg

PORTABLE / SUPERFAST / VEGETARIAN

SPINACH-PASTA SALAD

Try replacing the spinach with arugula, dandelion greens, or other tender leaves.

½ cup (1.6 ounces) uncooked mini farfalle
1½ tablespoons extra-virgin olive oil
1 tablespoon white wine vinegar
½ teaspoon Dijon mustard
¼ teaspoon freshly ground black pepper
⅛ teaspoon salt
2 garlic cloves, minced
3 cups baby spinach
¼ cup chopped red onion

1. Cook pasta according to package directions. Drain. Rinse with cold water; drain.
2. Combine olive oil and next 5 ingredients (through garlic) in a large bowl, stirring well with a whisk. Add garlic vinaigrette, spinach, and onion to pasta. Yield: 4 servings (serving size: about ⅔ cup).

CALORIES 106; **FAT** 5.4g (sat 0.8g, mono 3.7g, poly 0.7g); **PROTEIN** 2.6g; **CARB** 12.3g; **FIBER** 1.2g; **CHOL** 0mg; **IRON** 1.2mg; **SODIUM** 108mg; **CALC** 31mg

SUPERFAST / VEGETARIAN

SPICY PASTA-CUCUMBER SALAD ➤

Look for miso in the refrigerated part of the produce section or with the dairy products.

3 tablespoons sesame seeds, toasted
2 tablespoons white miso (soybean paste) or lower-sodium soy sauce
1 tablespoon rice vinegar
1 tablespoon honey
1 tablespoon hot water
1 teaspoon crushed red pepper
2 teaspoons dark sesame oil
¼ teaspoon salt
4 cups thinly sliced seeded cucumber
1 cup thinly sliced green onions
1 (9-ounce) package fresh linguine

1. Combine first 10 ingredients in a large bowl. Cut linguine into thirds; cook according to package directions. Drain; rinse with cold water. Toss pasta and cucumber mixture. Yield: 8 servings (serving size: about ¾ cup).

CALORIES 148; **FAT** 3.9g (sat 0.8g, mono 1.1g, poly 1.3g); **PROTEIN** 5.5g; **CARB** 24.3g; **FIBER** 2.7g; **CHOL** 19mg; **IRON** 1.8mg; **SODIUM** 223mg; **CALC** 59mg

MAKE-AHEAD / PORTABLE / VEGETARIAN

UDON NOODLE SALAD WITH BROCCOLINI AND SPICY TOFU

Blanching Broccolini in salted water keeps it crisp-tender, bright green, and full flavored. If you make the salad ahead, wait to dress it until just before serving to preserve the Broccolini's color.

8 ounces water-packed extra-firm tofu
5 tablespoons peanut oil, divided
2 tablespoons lower-sodium tamari or soy sauce
1½ teaspoons Sriracha (hot chile sauce), divided
Cooking spray
6 ounces uncooked dried udon noodles (thick, round Japanese wheat noodles)
6 cups water
1½ teaspoons kosher salt
8 ounces Broccolini
3 tablespoons rice wine vinegar
1 tablespoon grated peeled fresh ginger
1 teaspoon dark sesame oil
½ cup thinly sliced radishes (about 3 medium)
2 tablespoons chopped dry-roasted cashews, toasted

1. Cut tofu into ¾-inch-thick slices. Place tofu slices on several layers of paper towels; cover with additional paper towels. Let stand 30 minutes, pressing down occasionally. Remove tofu from paper towels, and cut into ¾-inch cubes.
2. Preheat oven to 350°.
3. Combine 2 tablespoons peanut oil, tamari, and 1 teaspoon Sriracha in a large bowl, stirring well with a whisk. Add tofu cubes to tamari mixture, and toss gently to coat. Let stand 15 minutes. Remove tofu from bowl with a slotted spoon; reserve tamari mixture in bowl. Arrange tofu in a single layer on a foil-lined baking sheet coated with cooking spray, and bake tofu at 350° for 10 minutes or until lightly golden.
4. Cook udon noodles according to package directions, omitting salt and fat. Drain and rinse with cold water; drain well.
5. Combine 6 cups water and salt in a large saucepan over high heat, and bring to a boil. Add Broccolini to pan; cook 3 minutes or until crisp-tender. Drain and plunge Broccolini into ice water; drain well. Chop Broccolini.
6. Add 3 tablespoons peanut oil, ½ teaspoon Sriracha, rice wine vinegar, ginger, and sesame oil to reserved tamari mixture in bowl; stir mixture well with a whisk. Add baked tofu, udon noodles, Broccolini, and ½ cup thinly sliced radishes to bowl; toss gently to coat. Sprinkle salad with cashews. Yield: 4 servings (serving size: 1¼ cups salad and 1½ teaspoons cashews).

CALORIES 438; **FAT** 24.7g (sat 4.1g, mono 10.1g, poly 8.2g); **PROTEIN** 14.3g; **CARB** 38.4g; **FIBER** 3.4g; **CHOL** 0mg; **IRON** 3mg; **SODIUM** 572mg; **CALC** 97mg

TOFU

For salads, choose regular (Momen or Chinese-style) tofu. Its dense texture makes it ideal to sauté, grill, bake, or broil.

THE GUIDE TO

BREADS

A SALAD IS A DELICIOUS way to give stale bread a second life: Breads can lend crunch and texture, soak up juices and dressings, and add flavor, too. Choose breads that are airy or have holes, rather than dense breads, when you want them to act as a crouton or take on flavors. Toasted or crisped pieces of flatbreads add crunch the way pita does in fattoush. Dense breads, like a baguette or sourdough bread, will add a chewy texture. Breads made with different grains will lend their flavor to the salad; corn bread, for example, gives panzanella a slightly sweet, Southern twist.

Stale bread is perfect for a salad. Because the texture is a little dry, it will absorb more liquid—and flavor—from the other salad ingredients. If you're starting with a fresh loaf, cube or slice the bread first, and toast it in the oven to dry it out slightly; then the bread will mimic its stale counterpart. Or grill slices of bread; the flame will dry the bread and give it a mild, charred flavor. Removing the crust is optional; without the crust, the bread will absorb dressings more evenly.

KID-FRIENDLY / MAKE-AHEAD / PORTABLE / VEGETARIAN

BELL PEPPER, TOMATO, CUCUMBER, AND GRILLED BREAD SALAD

Summer's freshest veggies combine in a colorful side-dish salad. Toss in grilled shrimp or chicken for an easy one-dish dinner.

4 (1-ounce) slices day-old country-style bread
4 cups coarsely chopped tomatoes (about 1½ pounds)
1 cup finely chopped red onion
¾ cup chopped yellow bell pepper
¾ cup chopped orange bell pepper
½ cup torn fresh basil leaves
1 English cucumber, peeled and coarsely chopped
¼ cup red wine vinegar
½ teaspoon freshly ground black pepper
¼ teaspoon salt
2 garlic cloves, minced
¼ cup extra-virgin olive oil

1. Preheat grill to medium-high heat.
2. Place bread slices on grill rack; grill 1 minute on each side or until golden brown with grill marks. Remove from grill; tear bread into 1-inch pieces.
3. Combine tomatoes, onion, bell peppers, basil, and cucumber in a large bowl. Add bread; toss gently.
4. Combine vinegar, black pepper, salt, and garlic in a small bowl, stirring with a whisk. Gradually add oil, stirring constantly with a whisk. Drizzle dressing over salad; toss gently to coat. Cover and chill 20 minutes before serving. Yield: 6 servings (serving size: 1⅔ cups).

CALORIES 178; **FAT** 9.7g (sat 1.3g, mono 6.6g, poly 1g); **PROTEIN** 3.5g; **CARB** 19.5g; **FIBER** 3.1g; **CHOL** 0mg; **IRON** 1.6mg; **SODIUM** 237mg; **CALC** 43mg

KID-FRIENDLY

BLT BREAD SALAD

Think of this hearty tossed salad as a deconstructed BLT sandwich, where the bread appears in the form of croutons. Round out the meal with a side of fresh cantaloupe.

6 ounces French bread baguette, cut into 1/2-inch cubes
Cooking spray
4 hickory-smoked bacon slices
1 tablespoon olive oil
1/4 cup red wine vinegar
1/4 teaspoon freshly ground black pepper
1/8 teaspoon salt
6 cups torn romaine lettuce
1 1/2 pounds plum tomatoes, cut into 1/2-inch wedges
3 thinly sliced green onions
1/2 cup (2 ounces) crumbled feta cheese

1. Preheat oven to 350°.
2. Layer bread on a baking sheet; coat with cooking spray. Bake at 350° for 18 minutes or until toasted.
3. Cook bacon in a large nonstick skillet over medium heat until crisp. Remove bacon from pan, reserving 1 tablespoon drippings in pan. Cut bacon into ½-inch pieces. Stir oil into bacon drippings in pan; remove from heat. Stir in vinegar, pepper, and salt.
4. Combine lettuce, tomatoes, and onions in a large bowl; drizzle with vinaigrette. Add bread; toss well to coat. Sprinkle with bacon and cheese. Serve immediately. Yield: 4 servings (serving size: about 2 cups).

CALORIES 319; **FAT** 15.2g (sat 5.4g, mono 6.6g, poly 2g); **PROTEIN** 12.1g; **CARB** 34.5g; **FIBER** 4.9g; **CHOL** 23mg; **IRON** 3mg; **SODIUM** 607mg; **CALC** 139mg

FETA

Greek feta is popular and best known for its salty, tangy flavor and versatility. French feta is packed in brine and has a smooth texture and flavor.

BREAD SALAD WITH CRANBERRIES, SPINACH, AND CHICKEN

Chicken teams up with spinach, nuts, and a little oil to offer a sweet and savory one-dish meal.

Chicken:

1 teaspoon ground fennel
1 teaspoon ground coriander
½ teaspoon kosher salt
⅛ teaspoon ground red pepper
4 (6-ounce) skinless, boneless chicken breast halves
4 teaspoons olive oil

Vinaigrette:

2 tablespoons thinly sliced shallots
5 garlic cloves, thinly sliced
¼ cup red wine vinegar
1 teaspoon grated orange rind
2 tablespoons orange juice
2 tablespoons cranberry juice
2 tablespoons honey
½ teaspoon ground fennel
½ teaspoon freshly ground black pepper
¼ teaspoon kosher salt

Remaining ingredients:

6 cups loosely packed spinach (about 6 ounces)
2½ cups (½-inch) cubed French bread, toasted (about 4 ounces)
½ cup dried sweetened cranberries
2 tablespoons pine nuts, toasted
2 tablespoons thinly sliced shallots
2 tablespoons sliced pitted kalamata olives

1. Combine first 4 ingredients; rub evenly over chicken. Heat a large nonstick skillet over medium heat. Add oil to pan; swirl to coat. Add chicken to pan; cook 5 minutes on each side or until done. Remove chicken from pan.

2. Add 2 tablespoons shallots and garlic to pan; cook 3 minutes or until shallots and garlic begin to brown, stirring occasionally. Stir in red wine vinegar, orange rind, juices, honey, ½ teaspoon fennel, black pepper, and ¼ teaspoon salt; cook over medium-high heat until reduced to ½ cup (about 1 minute). Remove vinaigrette from pan, and cool completely.

3. Chop chicken into bite-sized pieces. Combine chicken, spinach, and next 5 ingredients (through olives) in a large bowl. Drizzle vinaigrette over salad; toss gently to coat. Serve immediately. Yield: 6 servings (serving size: about 1⅔ cups).

CALORIES 307; **FAT** 8.2g (sat 1.1g, mono 4g, poly 1.7g); **PROTEIN** 29.5g; **CARB** 28.9g; **FIBER** 2.2g; **CHOL** 66mg; **IRON** 2.7mg; **SODIUM** 511mg; **CALC** 70mg

MAKE-AHEAD / PORTABLE

PANZANELLA

In spring, halved cherry tomatoes are your best bet for this salad. In summer, small fruit like the yellow pear tomatoes shown here or heirloom variety beefsteak tomatoes work well.

8 ounces ciabatta, cut into 1-inch cubes
2 orange bell peppers (about 1 pound)
2 cups sliced radicchio (about 4 ounces)
2 tablespoons capers, rinsed and drained
1 pound cherry or tear-drop cherry tomatoes, halved
1 medium cucumber, halved lengthwise, seeded, and sliced
3 tablespoons red wine vinegar
1½ teaspoons finely chopped canned anchovy fillets
½ teaspoon honey
¼ teaspoon salt
¼ teaspoon freshly ground black pepper
¼ cup extra-virgin olive oil
¼ cup torn fresh basil leaves

1. Preheat oven to 350°.
2. Place bread on a jelly-roll pan. Bake at 350° for 10 minutes or until crisp, stirring occasionally.
3. Preheat broiler.
4. Cut bell peppers in half lengthwise; discard seeds and membranes. Place pepper halves, skin sides up, on a foil-lined baking sheet; flatten with hand. Broil 10 minutes or until blackened. Place in a heavy-duty zip-top plastic bag; seal. Let stand 10 minutes. Peel; cut into 1-inch pieces.
5. Combine bread, bell peppers, and next 4 ingredients (through cucumber) in a large bowl. Combine vinegar and next 4 ingredients (through black pepper) in a small bowl. Gradually add oil, stirring with a whisk. Pour over bread mixture; toss.
6. Let stand 20 minutes or just until bread begins to soften. Sprinkle with basil. Yield: 10 servings (serving size: about 1 cup).

CALORIES 139; **FAT** 6.7g (sat 1g, mono 4.2g, poly 1.2g); **PROTEIN** 3.5g; **CARB** 17.2g; **FIBER** 1.9g; **CHOL** 1mg; **IRON** 1.2mg; **SODIUM** 229mg; **CALC** 39mg

HEIRLOOM TOMATOES

This fruit can come in colors ranging from off-white to brown to dark purple. Do not store tomatoes in the refrigerator; their sugars will quickly turn to starch and ruin their fabulous flavor.

KID-FRIENDLY / PORTABLE / SUPERFAST / VEGETARIAN

PITA SALAD WITH TOMATOES, CUCUMBER, AND HERBS

This recipe is similar to fattoush, a Lebanese bread salad. Traditionally, the bread is fried; here, it's crisped in the oven. Shredded cooked chicken converts it to a main course.

3 (7-inch) pitas
4 cups coarsely chopped romaine lettuce
2 cups diced English cucumber
2 cups halved cherry tomatoes
2/3 cup (about 3 ounces) crumbled feta cheese
1/2 cup thinly vertically sliced red onion
1/2 cup torn fresh mint leaves
1/4 cup thinly sliced green onions
1/4 cup finely chopped fresh flat-leaf parsley
6 tablespoons fresh lemon juice
1 teaspoon sugar
1 teaspoon freshly ground black pepper
1/4 teaspoon kosher salt
1/4 cup extra-virgin olive oil

1. Preheat oven to 375°.
2. Arrange pitas on a baking sheet. Bake at 375° for 14 minutes or until dry and crisp, turning after 7 minutes. Set aside; cool.
3. Combine lettuce and next 7 ingredients (through parsley) in a large bowl. Break pitas into bite-sized pieces. Add pitas to salad; toss gently to combine.
4. Combine juice, sugar, pepper, and salt in a small bowl; gradually add oil, stirring constantly with a whisk. Drizzle dressing over salad; toss well to coat. Let stand 30 minutes; serve at room temperature. Yield: 10 servings (serving size: 1 cup).

CALORIES 147; **FAT** 7.9g (sat 2.1g, mono 4.4g, poly 1g); **PROTEIN** 3.9g; **CARB** 16.2g; **FIBER** 1.9g; **CHOL** 8mg; **IRON** 1.1mg; **SODIUM** 256mg; **CALC** 83mg

THE GUIDE TO

BEANS

CANNED BEANS ARE A go-to pantry staple for salads and quick meals, but dried beans are more cost effective and allow you to control the amount of sodium, too. You can make a large pot of beans to use in meals throughout the week, and cooked beans also freeze well. Cooked, frozen beans are also available in stores and typically have less sodium than canned beans.

LENTILS
Tender and savory. Because of their small size and thin skins, lentils require no soaking and cook quickly. Some varieties, like French green, retain their shape better than others.

CANNELLINI *(white navy beans)*
Versatile with a delicate flavor and texture. Cook gently to avoid mushiness.

BLACK *(turtle beans)*
Versatile with white flesh and a slightly sweet flavo

BORLOTTI *(cranberry beans)*
Thin skins yield to a creamy texture with earthy flavo

FAVA
Emerald green (when fresh) with a firm texture and subtle nutty flavor. In season from late March to early May. Soak and cook dried favas (shown) before using them.

CHICKPEAS *(garbanzo beans)*
Nutty flavored; texture holds well when cooked.

MAKE-AHEAD / PORTABLE / VEGETARIAN

BLACK BEAN-QUINOA SALAD WITH BASIL-LEMON DRESSING

Quinoa contains more protein than any other grain. Edamame makes a tasty substitute for lima beans in this recipe. For an attractive presentation, serve the salad on a bed of baby greens or spinach.

1½ cups uncooked quinoa
3 cups lower-sodium vegetable broth
1 (14-ounce) package reduced-fat firm tofu, cut into ¼-inch cubes
3 tablespoons olive oil, divided
½ teaspoon salt, divided
1 cup chopped fresh basil
3 tablespoons fresh lemon juice
2 tablespoons Dijon mustard
1 teaspoon sugar
2 teaspoons grated lemon rind
½ teaspoon freshly ground black pepper
3 garlic cloves, minced
1 (10-ounce) package frozen baby lima beans
4 cups chopped tomato (about 3 medium)
½ cup sliced green onions
½ cup chopped carrot
1 (15-ounce) can black beans, rinsed and drained

1. Combine quinoa and vegetable broth in a saucepan; bring to a boil over medium-high heat. Cover, reduce heat, and simmer 15 minutes or until broth is absorbed and quinoa is tender. Remove from heat.

2. Place tofu on several layers of paper towels; cover with additional paper towels. Let stand 5 minutes. Heat a large nonstick skillet over medium-high heat. Add 1 tablespoon oil to pan; swirl to coat. Add tofu; sprinkle with ¼ teaspoon salt. Sauté tofu 9 minutes or until lightly browned. Remove from heat; cool completely.

3. Combine 2 tablespoons oil, ¼ teaspoon salt, basil, and next 6 ingredients (through garlic) in a large bowl; stir with a whisk until blended. Stir in quinoa.

4. Cook lima beans according to package directions, omitting salt and fat. Cool completely. Add lima beans, tofu, chopped tomato, green onions, chopped carrot, and black beans to quinoa mixture; stir gently to combine. Store, covered, in refrigerator until ready to serve. Yield: 6 servings (serving size: 1⅔ cups).

CALORIES 403; **FAT** 11.4g (sat 1.5g, mono 5.9g, poly 2.6g); **PROTEIN** 19.2g; **CARB** 56.9g; **FIBER** 11.6g; **CHOL** 0mg; **IRON** 5.6mg; **SODIUM** 539mg; **CALC** 224mg

MAKE-AHEAD / PORTABLE / VEGETARIAN

GRILLED PEPPERS AND LENTIL SALAD

You can substitute 1¼ teaspoons ground fennel seeds if fennel pollen is unavailable. Use any combination of sweet bell peppers you like: green, red, yellow, orange, or purple.

1 red bell pepper, quartered and seeded
1 yellow bell pepper, quartered and seeded
1 orange bell pepper, quartered and seeded
Cooking spray
1⅛ teaspoons salt, divided
½ teaspoon freshly ground black pepper, divided
1½ cups dried lentils (about ¾ pound)
1 small onion, peeled and halved
1 bay leaf
⅔ cup chopped plum tomato
½ cup diagonally cut green onions
⅓ cup fresh cilantro leaves
⅓ cup fresh lime juice
¼ cup chopped pitted kalamata olives
3 tablespoons extra-virgin olive oil
1 teaspoon fennel pollen

1. Preheat grill to high heat.
2. Lightly coat bell pepper pieces with cooking spray. Place bell pepper pieces, skin sides down, on grill rack; grill 12 minutes or until skins are blackened. Place bell pepper pieces in a zip-top plastic bag; seal. Let stand 15 minutes; peel and chop bell peppers. Discard skins. Sprinkle with ½ teaspoon salt and ¼ teaspoon freshly ground black pepper. Place bell peppers in a large bowl.
3. Rinse and drain lentils; place in a large saucepan. Cover with water to 3 inches above lentils; add onion and bay leaf to pan. Bring to a boil. Cover, reduce heat, and simmer 20 minutes or until lentils are just tender. Drain lentils. Discard onion halves and bay leaf. Add lentils to bell peppers. Combine lentil mixture, ⅝ teaspoon salt, ¼ teaspoon pepper, tomato, and remaining ingredients; stir well. Yield: 6 servings (serving size: 1⅓ cups).

CALORIES 287; **FAT** 8.8g (sat 1.1g, mono 5g, poly 1.1g); **PROTEIN** 15.7g; **CARB** 41g; **FIBER** 8.4g; **CHOL** 0mg; **IRON** 5mg; **SODIUM** 596mg; **CALC** 22mg

BELL PEPPERS

Like so many vegetables these days, bell peppers are now available year-round in supermarkets, thanks in part to imports from Mexico and Holland. But nothing beats a homegrown bell pepper at the peak of the growing season—which runs from July through November—when it's crisp, juicy, and full of sharp flavor.

VEGETARIAN

TOASTED CHICKPEA AND APRICOT SALAD

Plums are delicious—and beautiful—in place of apricots.

3 cups cooked or canned chickpeas, rinsed, drained, and patted dry
2 teaspoons ground cumin
1 teaspoon ground coriander
1/4 cup olive oil, divided
1 teaspoon grated orange rind
1 1/2 tablespoons white wine vinegar
1 1/2 tablespoons fresh orange juice
1/4 teaspoon kosher salt
1/4 teaspoon freshly ground black pepper
1/2 cup thinly vertically sliced red onion
4 large apricots, pitted and sliced
4 cups baby arugula leaves
1/2 cup (2 ounces) crumbled feta cheese

1. Preheat oven to 450°.
2. Combine first 3 ingredients in a roasting pan, and drizzle with 2 tablespoons oil, shaking pan to coat beans. Roast at 450° for 20 minutes, stirring once.
3. Combine 2 tablespoons oil, rind, vinegar, juice, salt, and pepper in a large bowl, stirring with a whisk. Stir in onion and apricots, tossing gently to coat. Add warm beans and arugula, tossing to combine. Sprinkle with cheese. Yield: 4 servings (serving size: about 1 2/3 cups salad and 2 tablespoons cheese).

CALORIES 340; **FAT** 19.3g (sat 4g, mono 10.7g, poly 1.6g); **PROTEIN** 10.9g; **CARB** 32.8g; **FIBER** 7.4g; **CHOL** 13mg; **IRON** 3mg; **SODIUM** 567mg; **CALC** 150mg

MAKE-AHEAD / PORTABLE
SUPERFAST / VEGETARIAN

MANGO AND BLACK BEAN SALAD

Canned beans are a great option for working protein and fiber into dishes. Organic, no-salt-added beans help keep sodium in check. The sweet mango brightens the earthiness of the beans and wild rice. Garnish with fresh cilantro. Serve with spicy pork tenderloins.

1 1/2 cups chopped peeled ripe mango
1 cup thinly sliced green onions
1/2 cup cooked wild or brown rice
3 tablespoons finely chopped fresh cilantro
2 tablespoons roasted tomatillo or fresh salsa
2 tablespoons fresh lime juice
2 tablespoons extra-virgin olive oil
3/4 teaspoon salt
1/4 teaspoon freshly ground black pepper
1 (15-ounce) can organic no-salt-added black beans, rinsed and drained

1. Combine all ingredients in a large bowl. Toss gently to mix. Yield: 6 servings (serving size: 2/3 cup).

CALORIES 167; **FAT** 5.4g (sat 0.7g, mono 3.4g, poly 0.8g); **PROTEIN** 5.2g; **CARB** 25.5g; **FIBER** 5.5g; **CHOL** 0mg; **IRON** 1.1mg; **SODIUM** 226mg; **CALC** 41mg

THE GUIDE TO

GRAINS

Enjoy cooked grains in salads for their chewy, satisfying texture. Because grains have a subtle taste, they provide a base for delicious salads by absorbing flavors from dressings and juices.

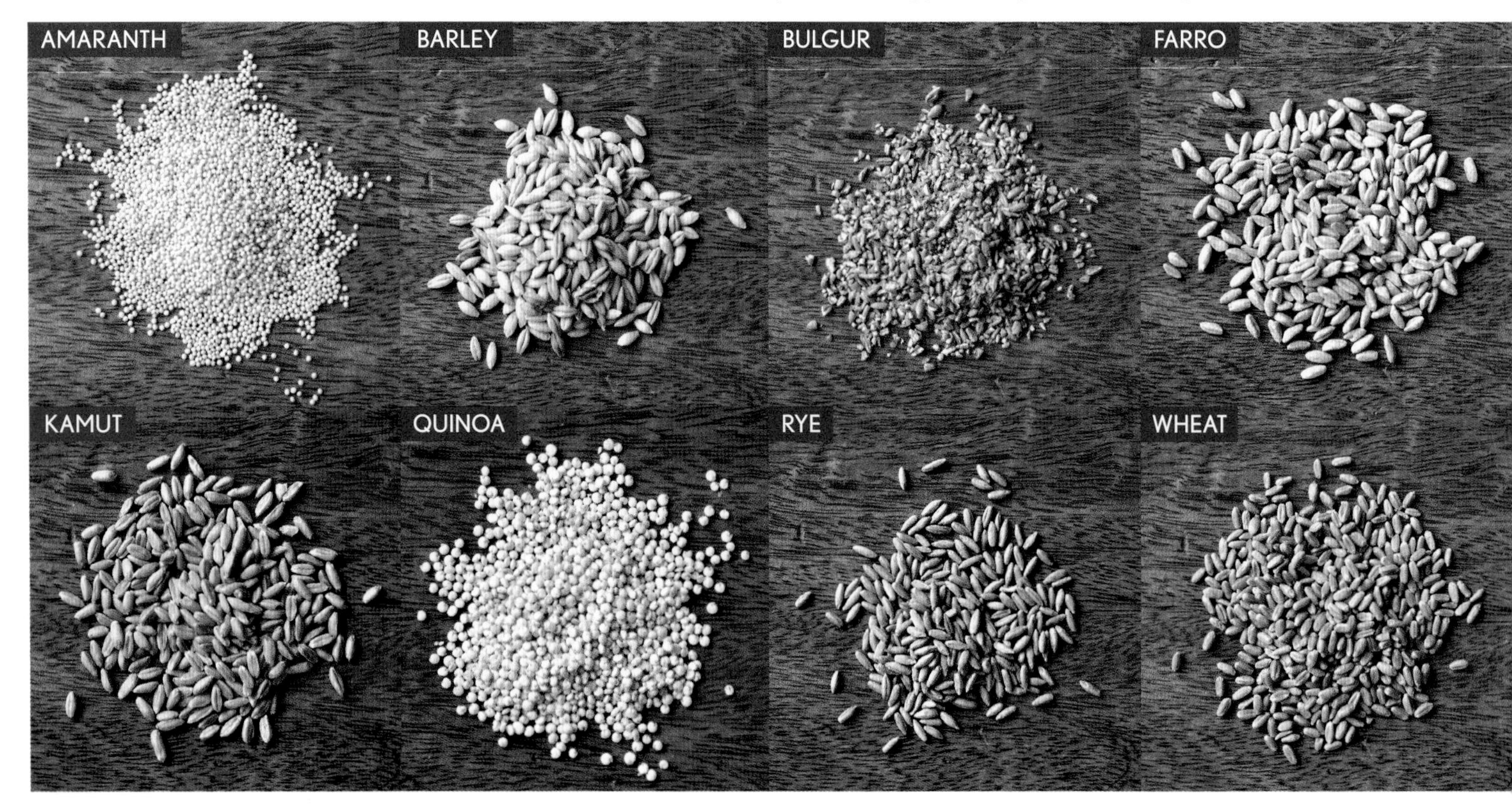

AMARANTH *[AM-ah-ranth]*
Amaranth was a principle food of the Aztecs. It has a slightly peppery, molasses-like flavor with a faint nuttiness. The grains (or seeds) are tiny, shiny, and can be yellow or black.

BARLEY
Barley is best known as an ingredient in beer and soup. Creamy with a fairly neutral flavor when cooked, pearl barley is easy to serve in place of rice. Whole barley, with its protective layer of bran intact, plumps nicely when cooked. A great source of fiber, ½ cup of pearl barley offers more than 12 grams.

BULGUR
Bulgur is wheat that has been steamed whole, dried, and then cracked. So bulgur is essentially precooked and quick to prepare; it needs only to be soaked to become tender.

FARRO
An ancient grain first grown in Egypt, farro is related to wheat. This grain is making a comeback, and commercial crops are grown in Italy. It cooks a little faster than wheat berries.

KAMUT *[kah-MOOT]*
Kamut berries are about twice the size of, but similar in flavor and texture to, wheat berries. Substitute kamut for wheat berries, and buy kamut flour to use in place of or alongside wheat flour.

QUINOA *[KEEN-wah]*
Quinoa is a good alternative to rice because of its lightness. The tiny seeds cook in about 20 minutes. Be sure to give quinoa a good rinse before cooking.

RYE
Whole rye berries are green and work nicely in salads. Rye berries are similar to wheat berries and kamut berries, and they hold their shape when cooked.

WHEAT
Wheat berries are simply whole-grain wheat. They are big, chewy, and take about an hour to cook.

MAKE-AHEAD / PORTABLE / VEGETARIAN

BEET, BLOOD ORANGE, KUMQUAT, AND QUINOA SALAD

Here, vibrant colors and winter flavor combine with rich sweetness from beets and bright acidity from orange and lemon. If you can't find blood oranges, substitute regular oranges.

Dressing:

1/4 cup finely chopped green onions
2 teaspoons grated blood orange rind
1 teaspoon grated lemon rind
2 tablespoons fresh blood orange juice
1 tablespoon fresh lemon juice
2 teaspoons finely chopped fresh cilantro
1/4 teaspoon salt
1/4 teaspoon ground coriander
1/4 teaspoon ground cumin
1/4 teaspoon paprika
3 tablespoons extra-virgin olive oil

Salad:

1 cup uncooked quinoa
1 3/4 cups water
1/2 teaspoon salt, divided
1 cup blood orange sections, chopped (about 4 medium)
1 cup diced peeled avocado
6 whole kumquats, seeded and sliced
2 medium beets, cooked and cut into wedges

1. To prepare dressing, combine first 10 ingredients in a medium bowl, stirring with a whisk. Gradually add oil, stirring constantly with a whisk. Set aside.
2. To prepare salad, place quinoa in a fine sieve, and place sieve in a large bowl. Cover quinoa with water. Using your hands, rub grains together for 30 seconds; rinse and drain. Repeat procedure twice. Drain well.
3. Combine 1¾ cups water, quinoa, and ¼ teaspoon salt in a medium saucepan; bring to a boil. Cover, reduce heat, and simmer 10 minutes or until liquid is absorbed. Remove from heat; fluff with a fork. Combine quinoa, ¼ teaspoon salt, blood orange sections, avocado, and kumquats in a large bowl, tossing gently to combine. Add dressing; toss gently to coat salad. Spoon 1 cup salad onto each of 4 plates; top each serving with about ½ cup beets. Yield: 4 servings.

CALORIES 442; **FAT** 20.7g (sat 2.7g, mono 12.3g, poly 2.1g); **PROTEIN** 9.1g; **CARB** 58g; **FIBER** 10.7g; **CHOL** 0mg; **IRON** 3.9mg; **SODIUM** 486mg; **CALC** 117mg

MAKE-AHEAD / PORTABLE / VEGETARIAN

BULGUR SALAD WITH EDAMAME AND CHERRY TOMATOES

Round out the meal with grilled chicken, lemony hummus, and toasted 100 percent whole-wheat pita wedges. Substitute fresh-shelled fava beans for edamame, if you like. Fava beans supply protein, fiber, and B vitamins. The vitamin C from lemon juice aids iron absorption.

1 cup uncooked bulgur
1 cup boiling water
1 cup frozen shelled edamame (green soybeans)
1 pound yellow and red cherry tomatoes, halved
1 cup finely chopped fresh flat-leaf parsley
1/3 cup finely chopped fresh mint
2 tablespoons chopped fresh dill
1 cup chopped green onions
1/4 cup fresh lemon juice
1/4 cup extra-virgin olive oil
1 teaspoon kosher salt
1/2 teaspoon freshly ground black pepper

1. Combine bulgur and 1 cup boiling water in a large bowl. Cover and let stand 30 minutes or until bulgur is tender.
2. Cook edamame in boiling water 3 minutes or until crisp-tender. Drain. Combine edamame, bulgur, tomatoes, and remaining ingredients; toss well. Let stand at room temperature 1 hour before serving. Yield: 6 servings (serving size: 1¼ cups).

CALORIES 208; **FAT** 10.5g (sat 1.3g, mono 6.7g, poly 1.2g); **PROTEIN** 6.3g; **CARB** 25.4g; **FIBER** 7.1g; **CHOL** 0mg; **IRON** 2.2mg; **SODIUM** 332mg; **CALC** 59mg

MAKE-AHEAD / PORTABLE / VEGETARIAN

BULGUR, MINT, AND PARSLEY SALAD

Light, herby, and vibrantly flavored, this salad makes a fine addition to a spread of Middle Eastern appetizers. Make up to two hours ahead so tastes can meld.

1 cup uncooked bulgur
1 cup boiling water
3 tablespoons fresh lemon juice
2 tablespoons extra-virgin olive oil
3 garlic cloves, minced
3 cups chopped tomato (about 2 large)
1 1/4 cups chopped seeded peeled cucumber (about 1 medium)
1 cup chopped fresh parsley
1/2 cup chopped green onions (about 3)
1/4 cup chopped fresh mint
3/4 teaspoon salt
1/2 teaspoon freshly ground black pepper

1. Combine bulgur and 1 cup boiling water in a medium bowl. Cover and let stand 30 minutes or until tender. Stir in juice, oil, and garlic. Cool to room temperature.
2. Combine bulgur mixture, tomato, and remaining ingredients in a large bowl; toss gently to coat. Yield: 8 servings (serving size: about 1 cup).

CALORIES 113; **FAT** 4g (sat 0.6g, mono 2.6g, poly 0.7g); **PROTEIN** 3.3g; **CARB** 18.4g; **FIBER** 4.7g; **CHOL** 0mg; **IRON** 1.3mg; **SODIUM** 234mg; **CALC** 36mg

MAKE-AHEAD / PORTABLE

CHICKEN AND WILD RICE SALAD WITH ALMONDS

The fig vinegar takes this dressing to a spectacular, unique level, but if you can't find it, you can substitute white wine vinegar.

Dressing:

1/4 cup fig vinegar or white wine vinegar
2 teaspoons sugar
1 teaspoon Dijon mustard
1/4 teaspoon salt
1 garlic clove, minced
2 tablespoons canola oil

Remaining ingredients:

2 cups fat-free, lower-sodium chicken broth
1 1/2 cups uncooked wild rice
1 tablespoon butter
Cooking spray
1 pound skinless, boneless chicken breast
1/4 teaspoon salt
1/8 teaspoon freshly ground black pepper
1 cup chopped celery
1/2 cup shredded carrot
1/3 cup dried cranberries
1/4 cup chopped almonds, toasted
2 tablespoons minced red onion

1. To prepare dressing, combine first 5 ingredients in a medium bowl. Gradually add oil, stirring with a whisk until well blended. Cover and chill.

2. Combine broth, rice, and butter in a medium saucepan; bring to a boil. Cover, reduce heat, and simmer 45 minutes or until rice is tender and liquid is absorbed. Remove rice mixture from heat; cool.

3. Heat a grill pan over medium-high heat. Coat pan with cooking spray. Sprinkle chicken with ¼ teaspoon salt and pepper. Add chicken to pan; cook 8 minutes on each side or until done. Cool; cut into ½-inch cubes.

4. Combine cooked rice, chicken, celery, carrot, cranberries, almonds, and red onion in a large bowl. Add dressing; toss gently to coat. Cover and chill. Yield: 6 servings (serving size: about 1⅓ cups).

CALORIES 352; **FAT** 10.3g (sat 2g, mono 5g, poly 2.5g); **PROTEIN** 25g; **CARB** 40.6g; **FIBER** 4g; **CHOL** 49mg; **IRON** 1.6mg; **SODIUM** 357mg; **CALC** 42mg

MAKE-AHEAD / VEGETARIAN

CURRIED QUINOA SALAD WITH CUCUMBER-MINT RAITA

Madras curry powder brings extra heat; use regular curry powder, if you'd prefer.

1 teaspoon olive oil
2 teaspoons Madras curry powder
1 garlic clove, crushed
1 cup uncooked quinoa
2 cups water
3/4 teaspoon kosher salt
1 diced peeled ripe mango
1/2 cup diced celery
1/4 cup thinly sliced green onions
3 tablespoons chopped fresh cilantro
3 tablespoons currants
1/4 cup finely diced peeled English cucumber
2 teaspoons chopped fresh mint
1 (6-ounce) carton plain low-fat yogurt
1 (5-ounce) package fresh baby spinach
Fresh cilantro leaves (optional)

1. Heat a medium saucepan over medium-high heat. Add oil to pan; swirl to coat. Add curry and garlic to pan; cook 1 minute, stirring constantly. Add quinoa and 2 cups water; bring to a boil. Cover, reduce heat, and simmer 16 minutes or until tender. Remove from heat; stir in salt. Cool completely.
2. Add mango, diced celery, thinly sliced green onions, chopped cilantro, and currants to cooled quinoa; toss gently.
3. Combine ¼ cup cucumber, 2 teaspoons mint, and yogurt in a small bowl, and stir well. Divide spinach evenly among 6 plates, and top each serving with about ¾ cup quinoa mixture, about 2 tablespoons raita, and fresh cilantro leaves, if desired. Yield: 6 servings.

CALORIES 268; **FAT** 4.5g (sat 0.9g, mono 1.9g, poly 1.3g); **PROTEIN** 10.7g; **CARB** 46.8g; **FIBER** 6g; **CHOL** 2mg; **IRON** 4.4mg; **SODIUM** 418mg; **CALC** 122mg

MAKE-AHEAD / PORTABLE / VEGETARIAN

CRACKED WHEAT SALAD WITH NECTARINES, PARSLEY, AND PISTACHIOS

Excellent with grilled chicken, lamb, or salmon for a party on the patio, this side-dish salad also packs well for a picnic. Almost any fruit would work in place of nectarines; try apricots, peaches, or figs.

1 cup uncooked bulgur
1 cup boiling water
1½ cups thinly sliced nectarines (about 3)
1/2 cup thinly sliced green onions
1/4 cup chopped fresh flat-leaf parsley
1 tablespoon chopped fresh dill
3 tablespoons extra-virgin olive oil
3 tablespoons white balsamic vinegar
1/2 teaspoon salt
1/4 teaspoon freshly ground black pepper
3 tablespoons chopped pistachios

1. Combine bulgur and 1 cup boiling water in a large bowl. Cover and let stand 1 hour.
2. Add nectarines and remaining ingredients except nuts to bulgur; toss well. Sprinkle with nuts. Yield: 6 servings (serving size: about ¾ cup).

CALORIES 185; **FAT** 9.2g (sat 1.3g, mono 6g, poly 1.7g); **PROTEIN** 4.1g; **CARB** 24.5g; **FIBER** 5.7g; **CHOL** 0mg; **IRON** 1.1mg; **SODIUM** 208mg; **CALC** 25mg

MAKE-AHEAD / VEGETARIAN

FARRO SALAD WITH ROASTED BEETS, WATERCRESS, AND POPPY SEED DRESSING

If you can't find farro, substitute wheat berries or spelt, but cook them a little longer.

2 bunches small beets, trimmed
2/3 cup uncooked farro
3 cups water
3/4 teaspoon kosher salt, divided
3 cups trimmed watercress
1/2 cup thinly sliced red onion
1/2 cup (2 ounces) crumbled goat cheese
2 tablespoons cider vinegar
2 tablespoons toasted walnut oil
2 tablespoons reduced-fat sour cream
1 1/2 teaspoons poppy seeds
2 teaspoons honey
1/2 teaspoon freshly ground black pepper
2 garlic cloves, crushed

1. Preheat oven to 375°.
2. Wrap beets in foil. Bake at 375° for 1½ hours or until tender. Cool; peel and thinly slice.
3. Place farro and 3 cups water in a medium saucepan; bring to a boil. Reduce heat, and simmer 25 minutes or until farro is tender. Drain and cool. Stir in ½ teaspoon salt.
4. Arrange 1½ cups watercress on a serving platter; top with half of farro, ¼ cup onion, and half of sliced beets. Repeat layers with 1½ cups watercress, remaining farro, ¼ cup onion, and remaining beets. Sprinkle with cheese.
5. Combine ¼ teaspoon salt, vinegar, and next 6 ingredients (through garlic); stir well with a whisk. Drizzle dressing over salad. Yield: 4 servings (serving size: about 1¾ cups salad and about 3 tablespoons dressing).

CALORIES 351; **FAT** 13.8g (sat 4.2g, mono 2.9g, poly 4.8g); **PROTEIN** 11.7g; **CARB** 50.3g; **FIBER** 5.1g; **CHOL** 14mg; **IRON** 3.8mg; **SODIUM** 604mg; **CALC** 140mg

COVER RECIPE

MAKE-AHEAD / PORTABLE

GREEK CHICKEN AND BARLEY SALAD

Dress up a Greek salad by adding barley to the cucumber, tomato, feta, and kalamata olives. The addition of chicken makes this a one-dish meal.

Salad:

2 (6-ounce) skinless, boneless chicken breast halves
1/8 teaspoon kosher salt
1 teaspoon olive oil
4 cups fat-free, lower-sodium chicken broth, divided
1 cup uncooked pearl barley
2 cups cubed seeded cucumber
1 cup grape tomatoes, halved
1/2 cup cubed yellow bell pepper
1/3 cup (about 1 1/2 ounces) reduced-fat crumbled feta cheese
1/4 cup chopped pitted kalamata olives

Dressing:

3 tablespoons extra-virgin olive oil
1 teaspoon grated lemon rind
2 tablespoons fresh lemon juice
1 tablespoon minced fresh basil
1 teaspoon minced fresh thyme
1 teaspoon red wine vinegar
1/2 teaspoon kosher salt
3 garlic cloves, minced

1. To prepare salad, sprinkle chicken with 1/8 teaspoon salt. Heat a nonstick skillet over medium-high heat. Add 1 teaspoon oil to pan; swirl to coat. Add chicken; cook 2 minutes on each side or until browned. Add 1 cup broth; cover, reduce heat, and simmer 10 minutes or until done. Cool; shred chicken. Discard broth.

2. Bring 3 cups broth to a boil in a large saucepan; add barley. Cover, reduce heat, and simmer 35 minutes or until liquid is absorbed. Fluff with a fork. Cool. Combine chicken, barley, cucumber, and next 4 ingredients (through olives) in a large bowl.

3. To prepare dressing, combine 3 tablespoons oil, rind, and next 6 ingredients (through garlic); stir well. Add to barley mixture; toss well. Cover and chill. Yield: 8 servings (serving size: 1 cup).

CALORIES 230; **FAT** 9.8g (sat 2g, mono 5.7g, poly 1.1g); **PROTEIN** 18g; **CARB** 18.3g; **FIBER** 3.2g; **CHOL** 38mg; **IRON** 1.2mg; **SODIUM** 611mg; **CALC** 38mg

MAKE-AHEAD / PORTABLE / VEGETARIAN

MEDITERRANEAN BARLEY SALAD

This is a nice side dish with roast chicken or pork. Save leftovers for lunch; with pearl barley and beans, it's hearty and filling, perfect for a take-along meal.

2¼ cups water
¾ cup uncooked pearl barley
1½ teaspoons grated lemon rind
3 tablespoons fresh lemon juice
2 tablespoons extra-virgin olive oil
½ teaspoon Dijon mustard
1 cup thinly sliced fennel bulb (about 1 small bulb)
⅓ cup chopped fresh parsley
¼ cup finely chopped red onion
½ teaspoon kosher salt
½ teaspoon coarsely ground black pepper
8 pitted kalamata olives, halved
1 (15-ounce) can cannellini beans, rinsed and drained
½ cup chopped walnuts, toasted

1. Bring 2¼ cups water and barley to a boil in a saucepan. Cover, reduce heat, and simmer 25 minutes or until tender and liquid is almost absorbed. Cool to room temperature.
2. Combine lemon rind, lemon juice, olive oil, and mustard in a large bowl; stir well with a whisk. Add barley, fennel, and next 6 ingredients (through beans); toss gently. Cover and refrigerate 30 minutes. Garnish with walnuts just before serving. Yield: 10 servings (serving size: ½ cup salad and about 2 teaspoons nuts).

CALORIES 162; **FAT** 7.5g (sat 0.8g, mono 3.6g, poly 2.8g); **PROTEIN** 5.6g; **CARB** 19.9g; **FIBER** 5g; **CHOL** 0mg; **IRON** 1.3mg; **SODIUM** 207mg; **CALC** 36mg

MAKE-AHEAD / PORTABLE

QUINOA AND PISTACHIO SALAD WITH MOROCCAN PESTO

Pair with simple grilled chicken or fish. For a vegetarian entrée option, use organic vegetable broth and add one (15½-ounce) can of rinsed, drained chickpeas to ramp up the protein.

1 red bell pepper
1 cup uncooked quinoa
1 cup fat-free, lower-sodium chicken broth
½ cup water
½ cup fresh orange juice
⅓ cup coarsely chopped fresh cilantro
¼ cup extra-virgin olive oil
2 tablespoons coarsely chopped fresh flat-leaf parsley
3 tablespoons fresh lemon juice
½ teaspoon ground cumin
¼ teaspoon kosher salt
¼ teaspoon ground red pepper
2 large garlic cloves, coarsely chopped
12 oil-cured olives, pitted and chopped
¼ cup chopped pistachios

1. Preheat broiler.
2. Cut red bell pepper in half lengthwise; discard seeds and membranes. Place pepper halves, skin sides up, on a foil-lined baking sheet; flatten with hand. Broil 12 minutes or until blackened. Place in a zip-top plastic bag; seal. Let stand 10 minutes. Peel and chop.
3. Place quinoa, broth, ½ cup water, and juice in a large saucepan; bring to a boil. Cover, reduce heat, and simmer 12 minutes or until liquid is absorbed.
4. Place cilantro and next 7 ingredients (through garlic) in a food processor; process until smooth. Combine bell pepper, quinoa mixture, cilantro mixture, and olives in a large bowl. Sprinkle with nuts. Yield: 6 servings (serving size: ¾ cup).

CALORIES 263; **FAT** 15.8g (sat 2.2g, mono 8.3g, poly 2.4g); **PROTEIN** 5.8g; **CARB** 28.2g; **FIBER** 4g; **CHOL** 0mg; **IRON** 3.3mg; **SODIUM** 318mg; **CALC** 36mg

ARTICHOKES

Fresh artichokes are nutty, mild-flavored treats that are worth seeking out. They are at peak flavor in early spring. Look for olive-green artichokes that feel heavy for their size and have tightly closed leaves that squeak when you rub them together. If you see black streaks, that's a sign of frost damage, but it's nothing to worry about. (Some aficionados think these taste better.) Enjoy fresh artichokes the day you buy them, or store them in a plastic bag for two to three days.

MAKE-AHEAD / PORTABLE

QUINOA SALAD WITH ARTICHOKES AND PARSLEY

1 tablespoon olive oil
1 cup chopped spring or sweet onion
1/2 teaspoon chopped fresh thyme
1 (9-ounce) package frozen artichoke hearts, thawed
1 cup fat-free, lower-sodium chicken broth
1/2 cup uncooked quinoa
1 cup chopped fresh parsley
5 teaspoons grated lemon rind
1 1/2 tablespoons fresh lemon juice
1/4 teaspoon kosher salt

1. Heat a medium saucepan over medium-high heat. Add oil to pan; swirl to coat. Add onion and thyme; sauté 5 minutes or until onion is tender. Add artichokes; sauté 2 minutes or until thoroughly heated. Add broth and quinoa; bring to a simmer. Cover and cook 18 minutes or until liquid is completely absorbed.
2. Remove pan from heat. Stir in parsley, rind, juice, and salt. Serve warm or at room temperature. Yield: 8 servings (serving size: about 1/3 cup).

CALORIES 83; **FAT** 2.8g (sat 0.3g, mono 1.4g, poly 0.6g); **PROTEIN** 3g; **CARB** 12.4g; **FIBER** 3.5g; **CHOL** 0mg; **IRON** 1.2mg; **SODIUM** 135mg; **CALC** 39mg

MAKE-AHEAD / PORTABLE / VEGETARIAN

QUINOA SALAD WITH ASPARAGUS, DATES, AND ORANGE

Several international influences converge here: The dates and orange are an Israeli touch; the pecans pay homage to the American South; and the quinoa is from South America.

Salad:

1 teaspoon olive oil
½ cup finely chopped white onion
1 cup uncooked quinoa
2 cups water
½ teaspoon kosher salt
1 cup fresh orange sections (about 1 large orange)
¼ cup chopped pecans, toasted
2 tablespoons minced red onion
5 dates, pitted and chopped
½ pound (2-inch) slices asparagus, steamed and chilled
½ jalapeño pepper, diced

Dressing:

2 tablespoons fresh lemon juice
1 tablespoon extra-virgin olive oil
¼ teaspoon kosher salt
¼ teaspoon freshly ground black pepper
1 garlic clove, minced
2 tablespoons chopped fresh mint
Mint sprigs (optional)

1. To prepare salad, heat a large nonstick skillet over medium-high heat. Add 1 teaspoon oil; swirl to coat. Add white onion to pan; sauté 2 minutes. Add quinoa to pan; sauté 5 minutes. Add 2 cups water and ½ teaspoon salt to pan; bring to a boil. Cover, reduce heat, and simmer 15 minutes. Remove from heat; let stand 15 minutes or until water is absorbed. Transfer quinoa mixture to a large bowl. Add orange and next 5 ingredients (through jalapeño); toss gently to combine.
2. To prepare dressing, combine juice and next 4 ingredients (through garlic) in a small bowl, stirring with a whisk. Pour dressing over salad; toss gently to coat. Sprinkle with chopped mint. Garnish with mint sprigs, if desired. Serve at room temperature. Yield: 8 servings (serving size: ¾ cup).

CALORIES 164; **FAT** 6.3g (sat 0.7g, mono 3.5g, poly 1.7g); **PROTEIN** 4.3g; **CARB** 24.7g; **FIBER** 3.4g; **CHOL** 0mg; **IRON** 2.5mg; **SODIUM** 186mg; **CALC** 38mg

MAKE-AHEAD / PORTABLE

QUINOA SALAD WITH TOASTED PISTACHIOS AND DRIED PINEAPPLE

Fluffy quinoa offers a crunchy texture to this filling salad. Toast the quinoa before cooking if you prefer a nuttier flavor.

1½ cups water
¾ cup uncooked quinoa
¼ cup chopped shelled pistachios (about 1 ounce)
2 cups chopped skinless, boneless rotisserie chicken breast
⅓ cup chopped green onions
⅓ cup chopped dried pineapple
1 tablespoon toasted sesame oil
1½ teaspoons bottled ground fresh ginger
½ teaspoon ground cumin
½ teaspoon salt
¼ teaspoon crushed red pepper

1. Bring 1½ cups water to a boil in a small saucepan; add quinoa. Cover, reduce heat, and simmer 12 minutes.
2. Heat a small skillet over medium-high heat. Add chopped pistachios, and cook 2 minutes or until lightly toasted, stirring frequently. Transfer pistachios to a large bowl; add cooked quinoa, chicken, and remaining ingredients to bowl. Toss gently to coat. Yield: 4 cups (serving size: 1 cup).

CALORIES 344; **FAT** 10.7g (sat 1.6g, mono 4.7g, poly 3.7g); **PROTEIN** 27g; **CARB** 32.5g; **FIBER** 3.7g; **CHOL** 60mg; **IRON** 3.2mg; **SODIUM** 362mg; **CALC** 42mg

THE GUIDE TO

RICE

THERE ARE MORE THAN 40,000 varieties of rice. Which are best for salads? Long-grain rices have less starch than short-grain varieties, and the grains will stay separate and fluffy after they have been cooked. Save short-grain rices for sushi and risotto.

RED

This aromatic rice with reddish brown bran has a nutty flavor and a chewy consistency. Look for it in specialty markets Red rice is great with hearty ingredients like pork or butternut squash.

BROWN

This is rice that has been hulled with bran intact. The bran lends chewy texture and nutty flavor. It requires a longer cooking time because the bran is a barrier to water.

BASMATI

Sometimes called "popcorn rice," this long-grain variety is highly regarded for its fragrance, taste, and slender shape

WILD

The only grain native to North America, this is actually an aquatic grass. It's often sold mixed with long-grain white rice

MAKE-AHEAD / PORTABLE / VEGETARIAN

SPANISH RICE SALAD

Dressing:

1½ tablespoons extra-virgin olive oil
1 tablespoon fresh lemon juice
1 tablespoon red wine vinegar
1 teaspoon chopped fresh oregano
1 small garlic clove, minced

Salad:

½ cup uncooked medium-grain rice
1 tablespoon fresh lemon juice
2 large globe artichokes
¼ teaspoon salt
⅛ teaspoon freshly ground black pepper
¾ cup canned chickpeas (garbanzo beans), rinsed and drained
¼ cup finely chopped red onion
¼ cup diced piquillo peppers or roasted red bell peppers
1½ tablespoons chopped fresh flat-leaf parsley

1. To prepare dressing, combine first 5 ingredients in a small bowl, stirring well with a whisk. Set aside.
2. To prepare salad, cook rice according to package directions, omitting salt and fat.
3. Fill a medium bowl with cold water; stir in 1 tablespoon juice. Working with 1 artichoke at a time, cut off stem to within 1 inch of base. Peel stem. Remove bottom leaves and tough outer leaves, leaving tender heart and bottom. Cut artichoke in half lengthwise. Remove fuzzy thistle with a spoon. Slice artichoke heart into eighths; place in lemon water. Repeat with remaining artichoke. Drain.
4. Place artichokes in a saucepan; cover with water to 1 inch. Bring to a boil over medium-high heat; cook 10 minutes or until tender. Drain well.
5. Transfer rice to a large bowl; stir in salt and black pepper. Combine rice, dressing, artichokes, chickpeas, and remaining ingredients; stir well. Serve warm or at room temperature. Yield: 8 servings (serving size: ½ cup).

CALORIES 117; **FAT** 2.9g (sat 0.4g, mono 1.9g, poly 0.4g); **PROTEIN** 3.4g; **CARB** 20.1g; **FIBER** 3.5g; **CHOL** 0mg; **IRON** 1.4mg; **SODIUM** 192mg; **CALC** 30mg

MAKE-AHEAD / PORTABLE / VEGETARIAN

SPICY SOUTHWESTERN TABBOULEH

Use prechopped vegetables from the grocery store for a fast weeknight meal. If necessary, you can even soak the bulgur overnight.

3/4 cup uncooked bulgur
1 1/4 cups boiling water
1 1/2 teaspoons extra-virgin olive oil
1 cup chopped fresh cilantro
1 cup vertically sliced red onion
3/4 cup diced seeded tomato
1/2 cup sliced green onion bottoms (white part)
1/2 cup diced yellow bell pepper
1/2 cup chopped peeled avocado
1/4 cup diced seeded peeled cucumber
1/4 cup (1 ounce) crumbled queso fresco
1/4 cup extra-virgin olive oil
2 tablespoons fresh lemon juice
2 tablespoons fresh lime juice
2 teaspoons diced seeded jalapeño pepper
3/4 teaspoon dried oregano
1/2 teaspoon salt
1/4 teaspoon ground cumin
1/4 teaspoon ground red pepper
1/4 teaspoon paprika
1/4 teaspoon chili powder
1/4 teaspoon freshly ground black pepper
1/8 teaspoon ground allspice
1 garlic clove, minced
Dash of hot pepper sauce
4 green onion tops, cut into 2-inch julienne strips (optional)

1. Combine bulgur, 1¼ cups boiling water, and 1½ teaspoons oil in a medium bowl; cover and let stand 30 minutes or until tender.
2. Drain bulgur through a fine sieve; place bulgur in a medium bowl. Add cilantro and next 21 ingredients (through pepper sauce); toss well. Add green onion tops, if desired.
Yield: 6 servings (serving size: ¾ cup).

CALORIES 212; **FAT** 13.7g (sat 2.4g, mono 9g, poly 1.9g); **PROTEIN** 4.6g; **CARB** 21.1g; **FIBER** 5.4g; **CHOL** 3mg; **IRON** 1.1mg; **SODIUM** 224mg; **CALC** 61mg

CILANTRO

Also called Chinese parsley and coriander (the dried spice coriander comes from cilantro plants), cilantro's leaves, stems, and roots are all flavorful. Wrap fresh cilantro in barely damp paper towels, place in a plastic bag, and store in the warmest part of the fridge.

MAKE-AHEAD / PORTABLE / VEGETARIAN

SUMMER BARLEY SALAD

Try this colorful salad and buttery lemon green beans as summery sides for a cookout.

1½ cups uncooked pearl barley
1 cup fresh corn kernels (about 2 ears)
1 cup diced seeded plum tomato (about 2 small)
½ cup chopped green onions
¼ cup chopped fresh flat-leaf parsley
15 kalamata olives, pitted and coarsely chopped
3 tablespoons fresh lemon juice
2 tablespoons olive oil
¼ teaspoon salt
¼ teaspoon freshly ground black pepper
1 garlic clove, minced
½ cup (2 ounces) crumbled feta cheese

1. Cook barley according to package directions, omitting salt. Drain and rinse with cold water; drain. Cool completely. Combine barley, corn, and next 4 ingredients (through kalamata olives) in a large bowl. Combine juice and next 4 ingredients (through garlic), stirring well with a whisk; drizzle over barley mixture. Toss to coat. Sprinkle with cheese. Yield: 4 servings (serving size: about 1 cup).

CALORIES 454; **FAT** 15.2g (sat 3.8g, mono 8.8g, poly 2.2g); **PROTEIN** 11.6g; **CARB** 71.9g; **FIBER** 14.1g; **CHOL** 13mg; **IRON** 2.8mg; **SODIUM** 557mg; **CALC** 121mg

MAKE-AHEAD / PORTABLE / VEGETARIAN

SUMMER PEA, WATERMELON, AND FARRO SALAD ➤

1 cup uncooked farro or wheat berries
1 cup shelled green peas (about ¾ pound unshelled)
½ teaspoon salt
¼ teaspoon freshly ground black pepper
1 cup cubed seeded watermelon
1 cup coarsely chopped fresh flat-leaf parsley
⅓ cup (about 1½ ounces) shaved fresh pecorino Romano cheese

1. Place farro in a large saucepan, and cover with water to 2 inches above farro. Bring to a boil. Cover, reduce heat, and simmer 23 minutes or until desired degree of doneness.
2. Add green peas to pan with farro, and cook 2 minutes or until crisp-tender. Drain and rinse farro mixture with cold water; drain.
3. Combine farro mixture, ½ teaspoon salt, and ¼ teaspoon black pepper in a large bowl. Add watermelon cubes and 1 cup chopped parsley, and toss gently to combine. Top salad with cheese. Yield: 4 servings (serving size: 1 cup).

CALORIES 188; **FAT** 4.2g (sat 1.9g, mono 0.9g, poly 0.2g); **PROTEIN** 10g; **CARB** 35.5g; **FIBER** 6g; **CHOL** 11mg; **IRON** 1.7mg; **SODIUM** 433mg; **CALC** 146mg

TOASTED BARLEY, GREEN BEAN, AND SHIITAKE SALAD WITH TOFU

Toasting the barley before it boils brings out its nutty flavor. Pressing and draining tofu helps it take on flavors more readily and improves its cooked texture.

Tofu:

1 (12-ounce) package extra-firm tofu, drained and cut into 5 (1-inch-thick) slices
1 tablespoon brown sugar
2 tablespoons lower-sodium soy sauce
1 teaspoon grated peeled fresh ginger
1 teaspoon dark sesame oil
1 garlic clove, grated
Cooking spray

Salad:

2 tablespoons dark sesame oil, divided
1 cup uncooked pearl barley
5 cups water
1/2 teaspoon salt, divided
1 pound green beans, trimmed and cut into 2-inch pieces
10 ounces large shiitake mushrooms, stems removed
1 1/2 cups thinly sliced green onions
1/4 cup rice wine vinegar
2 tablespoons lower-sodium soy sauce
2 tablespoons agave nectar or honey
2 teaspoons finely grated peeled fresh ginger
1 garlic clove, minced

1. To prepare tofu, place tofu slices on several layers of paper towels; cover with additional paper towels. Let stand 45 minutes, pressing down occasionally. Cut each tofu slice into 10 cubes; arrange in a single layer in a shallow dish.
2. Preheat oven to 375°.
3. Combine brown sugar and next 4 ingredients (through garlic) in a small bowl. Pour sugar mixture over tofu in dish, and turn to coat. Let stand 25 minutes. Arrange tofu in a single layer on a baking sheet coated with cooking spray. Bake at 375° for 35 minutes, turning after 15 minutes. Cool completely.
4. To prepare salad, heat a heavy saucepan over medium-high heat. Add 1 teaspoon sesame oil to pan; swirl to coat. Add barley to pan; cook 3 minutes or until lightly toasted, stirring frequently. Add 5 cups water and ¼ teaspoon salt; bring to a boil. Reduce heat, and simmer 45 minutes or until barley is tender. Drain; cool completely. Place barley in a large bowl.
5. Cook green beans in boiling water 4 minutes or until crisp-tender. Drain and plunge green beans into ice water. Drain well; pat dry. Add beans to barley.
6. Heat a grill pan over medium-high heat. Brush tops of mushrooms with 2 teaspoons oil. Add mushrooms to pan, oiled side down. Cook 5 minutes or until browned. Sprinkle evenly with ¼ teaspoon salt. Cool slightly; slice mushrooms thinly. Add tofu, mushrooms, and green onions to barley mixture.
7. Combine 1 tablespoon oil, rice wine vinegar, and next 4 ingredients (through garlic) in a small bowl, stirring with a whisk. Drizzle over barley mixture in bowl; stir well to combine. Serve at room temperature or chilled. Yield: 6 servings (serving size: about 1½ cups).

CALORIES 302; **FAT** 9.2g (sat 1.2g, mono 3.1g, poly 4.1g); **PROTEIN** 11.3g; **CARB** 46.8g; **FIBER** 10.2g; **CHOL** 0mg; **IRON** 3.2mg; **SODIUM** 577mg; **CALC** 102mg

GREEN BEANS

To choose good beans, look closely. If the sides of the pods are bulging from the seeds, the beans will be tough because they were picked too late. Make sure the skin is taut. Next, pick up a bean, and break it in half. If you hear the signature snap, the bean is fresh.

MAKE-AHEAD / PORTABLE / VEGETARIAN

WHEAT BERRY SALAD WITH GOAT CHEESE

Taking a cue from traditional tabbouleh, this dish uses lots of peak-season vegetables, tart lemon juice, and pungent fresh herbs. Serve with toasted pita wedges or favorite crackers.

1¼ cups uncooked wheat berries (hard winter wheat)
2½ cups chopped English cucumber
⅔ cup thinly sliced green onions
1½ cups loosely packed chopped arugula
6 tablespoons minced fresh flat-leaf parsley
1 pint grape tomatoes, halved
1 tablespoon grated lemon rind
3 tablespoons fresh lemon juice
1 teaspoon kosher salt
½ teaspoon freshly ground black pepper
½ teaspoon sugar
2 tablespoons extra-virgin olive oil
¾ cup (3 ounces) crumbled goat cheese

1. Place wheat berries in a medium bowl; cover with water to 2 inches above wheat berries. Cover and let stand 8 hours. Drain.
2. Place wheat berries in a medium saucepan; cover with water to 2 inches above wheat berries. Bring to a boil, reduce heat, and cook, uncovered, 1 hour or until tender. Drain and rinse with cold water; drain well. Place wheat berries in a large bowl; add cucumber and next 4 ingredients (through tomatoes).
3. Combine rind and next 4 ingredients (through sugar) in a bowl; gradually add oil, stirring constantly with a whisk. Drizzle dressing over salad; toss well to coat. Stir in cheese. Let stand at least 30 minutes; serve at room temperature. Yield: 6 servings (serving size: about 1⅓ cups).

CALORIES 253; **FAT** 9.7g (sat 3.7g, mono 4.4g, poly 0.9g); **PROTEIN** 9.2g; **CARB** 35.7g; **FIBER** 6.8g; **CHOL** 11mg; **IRON** 1.2mg; **SODIUM** 401mg; **CALC** 79mg

GOAT CHEESE

Loved for its characteristic acidic flavor, goat cheese ranges from soft and spreadable to dry and crumbly. Store in the refrigerator for up to two weeks.

MAKE-AHEAD / PORTABLE / VEGETARIAN

WHEAT BERRY SALAD WITH RAISINS AND PISTACHIOS

Whole-grain wheat berries are chewy, mild, and packed with fiber. Prep all the ingredients while the grain cooks.

1 cup uncooked wheat berries (hard winter wheat)
3/4 teaspoon salt, divided
3 tablespoons shelled pistachios
2 tablespoons olive oil
2 tablespoons fresh lemon juice
2 teaspoons honey
1/2 teaspoon ground coriander
1/2 teaspoon grated peeled fresh ginger
1/2 cup golden raisins
1/4 cup thinly sliced green onions
2 tablespoons chopped fresh cilantro
1/2 cup (2 ounces) crumbled goat cheese

1. Preheat oven to 350°.
2. Place wheat berries and ½ teaspoon salt in a medium saucepan. Cover with water to 2 inches above wheat berries, and bring to a boil. Cover, reduce heat to medium-low, and simmer 1 hour or until tender. Drain.
3. While wheat berries cook, place pistachios on a baking sheet. Bake at 350° for 8 minutes, stirring once. Cool slightly, and chop.
4. Combine oil, juice, honey, coriander, ginger, and ¼ teaspoon salt in a large bowl, stirring with a whisk. Add hot wheat berries and raisins; stir well to combine. Let stand 20 minutes or until cooled to room temperature.
5. Add nuts, ¼ cup green onions, and cilantro to wheat berry mixture. Transfer to a serving bowl, and sprinkle with goat cheese. Yield: 6 servings (serving size: about ½ cup).

CALORIES 240; **FAT** 8.9g (sat 2.3g, mono 4.8g, poly 1.3g); **PROTEIN** 7.2g; **CARB** 36.8g; **FIBER** 5g; **CHOL** 4mg; **IRON** 0.7mg; **SODIUM** 284mg; **CALC** 28mg

poultry & meats

Change your weeknight dinner routine and jazz up lunch with these filling salads: Combine favorite ingredients in fresh ways for satisfying meals that hit the spot.

ARUGULA SALAD WITH CHICKEN AND APRICOTS, p. 178 →

SUPERFAST

ARUGULA SALAD WITH CHICKEN AND APRICOTS

2 (6-ounce) skinless, boneless chicken breast halves
1 tablespoon minced fresh parsley
2 teaspoons minced fresh tarragon
½ teaspoon salt, divided
¼ teaspoon freshly ground black pepper
Cooking spray
3 tablespoons olive oil
4 teaspoons white wine vinegar
Dash of freshly ground black pepper
4 cups baby arugula
4 cups gourmet salad greens
3 apricots (about 8 ounces), pitted and thinly sliced
⅓ cup thinly vertically sliced red onion

1. Preheat grill to medium-high heat.
2. Place chicken between 2 sheets of heavy-duty plastic wrap; pound each piece to ½-inch thickness using a meat mallet or small heavy skillet. Sprinkle chicken with parsley, tarragon, ¼ teaspoon salt, and ¼ teaspoon pepper.
3. Place chicken on grill rack coated with cooking spray; grill 4 minutes on each side or until done. Transfer to a plate; cool to room temperature.
4. Combine oil, vinegar, ¼ teaspoon salt, and dash of pepper in a small bowl, stirring with a whisk.
5. Combine arugula, greens, apricots, and onion in a large bowl. Pour vinaigrette over arugula mixture; toss well to coat. Arrange about 2 cups arugula mixture onto each of 4 plates. Cut chicken breast halves crosswise into thin slices; top each serving evenly with chicken. Serve immediately. Yield: 4 servings.

CALORIES 243; **FAT** 12.9g (sat 2.1g, mono 8.3g, poly 1.7g); **PROTEIN** 22.2g; **CARB** 10.1g; **FIBER** 2.9g; **CHOL** 54mg; **IRON** 2.1mg; **SODIUM** 364mg; **CALC** 86mg

KID-FRIENDLY / MAKE-AHEAD / PORTABLE

EASY GRILLED CHICKEN SALAD ➤

Serve this main-dish salad over fresh spinach. Regular spinach is the least expensive option, but you'll have to remove the stems. If time is your main concern, buy baby spinach.

4 (6-ounce) skinless, boneless chicken breast halves
1 tablespoon olive oil
½ teaspoon salt
½ teaspoon freshly ground black pepper
Cooking spray
⅓ cup finely chopped celery
⅓ cup sweetened dried cranberries
¼ cup chopped pecans, toasted
3 green onions, thinly sliced
¼ cup vertically sliced red onion (optional)
3 tablespoons light sour cream
3 tablespoons canola mayonnaise
2 teaspoons fresh lemon juice

1. Preheat grill to medium-high heat.
2. Brush both sides of chicken evenly with oil; sprinkle with salt and pepper. Place chicken on grill rack coated with cooking spray; grill 6 minutes on each side or until done. Let stand 10 minutes; shred. Place chicken in a large bowl. Add celery, next 3 ingredients (through green onions), and, if desired, red onion; toss.
3. Combine sour cream, mayonnaise, and juice, stirring well. Add sour cream mixture to chicken mixture; toss to coat. Yield: 4 servings (serving size: 1¼ cups).

CALORIES 391; **FAT** 22g (sat 3.4g, mono 11.4g, poly 5.1g); **PROTEIN** 36.1g; **CARB** 11.5g; **FIBER** 1.8g; **CHOL** 101mg; **IRON** 1.6mg; **SODIUM** 469mg; **CALC** 59mg

100-CALORIE SALAD BOOSTERS

Start with 1½ cups of fresh mixed greens. Add a tablespoon of your favorite vinaigrette. Then pile on the good stuff. Add some Asian flavor with this low-calorie combo.

1 TABLESPOON CHOPPED ROASTED PEANUTS

2 TABLESPOONS EDAMAME

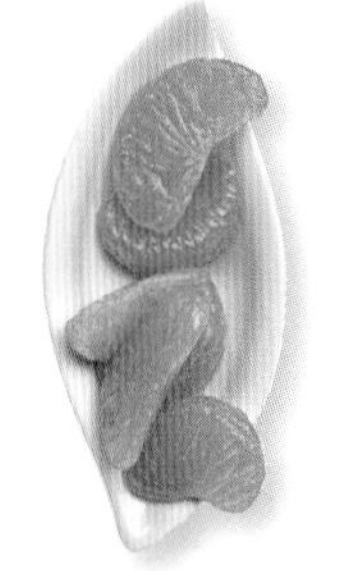

2 TABLESPOONS MANDARIN ORANGE SECTIONS

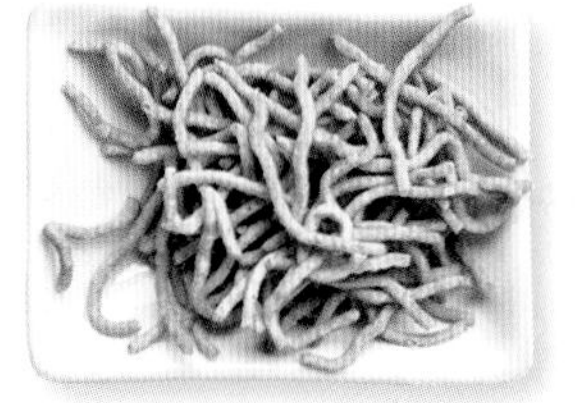

1 TABLESPOON CRUNCHY CHINESE NOODLES

CHICKEN AND GLASS NOODLE SALAD

To ensure the noodles get soft, soak them in the hottest water you can get from your tap. The salad is moderately spicy; reduce the chile paste by 1 teaspoon, or omit it for a milder dish.

1 (3.75-ounce) package uncooked bean threads (cellophane noodles)
2 tablespoons rice vinegar
2 tablespoons fresh lime juice
1½ tablespoons fish sauce
1 teaspoon sugar
2 teaspoons sambal oelek (ground fresh chile paste)
2 cups shredded skinless, boneless rotisserie chicken breast
½ cup matchstick-cut or grated carrot
½ cup red bell pepper strips
⅓ cup thinly sliced shallots
2 tablespoons fresh cilantro leaves
1 tablespoon chopped fresh mint
½ cup chopped unsalted, dry-roasted peanuts

1. Place noodles in a large bowl. Cover with very hot tap water, and let stand 15 minutes.
2. While noodles soak, combine vinegar and next 4 ingredients (through sambal oelek), stirring until sugar dissolves. Combine chicken and next 5 ingredients (through mint), tossing well.
3. Drain and rinse noodles with cold water; drain well, squeezing to remove excess water. Snip noodles several times with kitchen shears. Combine noodles and chicken mixture, tossing well to combine. Drizzle noodle mixture with vinegar mixture; toss well to coat. Top with peanuts. Yield: 4 servings (serving size: about 1½ cups salad and 2 tablespoons peanuts).

CALORIES 346; **FAT** 11.7g (sat 2g, mono 5.4g, poly 3.5g); **PROTEIN** 27.1g; **CARB** 34.1g; **FIBER** 2.4g; **CHOL** 60mg; **IRON** 2.1mg; **SODIUM** 589mg; **CALC** 44mg

KID-FRIENDLY / SUPERFAST

CHICKEN AND STRAWBERRY SALAD

Pair this easy, no-cook meal with toasted buttery baguette slices.

Dressing:

1 tablespoon sugar
2 tablespoons red wine vinegar
1 tablespoon water
1/8 teaspoon salt
1/8 teaspoon freshly ground black pepper
2 tablespoons extra-virgin olive oil

Salad:

4 cups torn romaine lettuce
4 cups arugula leaves
2 cups quartered strawberries
1/3 cup vertically sliced red onion
12 ounces skinless, boneless rotisserie chicken breast, sliced
2 tablespoons unsalted cashews, halved
1/2 cup (2 ounces) crumbled blue cheese

1. To prepare dressing, combine first 5 ingredients in a small bowl. Gradually drizzle in oil, stirring constantly with a whisk.
2. To prepare salad, combine romaine and next 4 ingredients (through chicken) in a bowl; toss gently. Arrange about 2 cups chicken mixture on each of 4 plates; top each serving with 1½ teaspoons cashews and 2 tablespoons cheese. Drizzle about 4 teaspoons dressing over each serving. Yield: 4 servings.

CALORIES 333; **FAT** 16.4g (sat 4.9g, mono 8.3g, poly 2.1g); **PROTEIN** 32g; **CARB** 14.8g; **FIBER** 3.5g; **CHOL** 83mg; **IRON** 2.5mg; **SODIUM** 347mg; **CALC** 156mg

STRAWBERRIES

When spring arrives, choose berries that are plump, deep red, and very fragrant. They should be firm without bruises, and the green stem leaves should be bright green and fresh looking. Buy organic if you can; strawberries can harbor pesticides even after washing.

KID-FRIENDLY

CHICKEN DINNER SALAD

Yogurt in the marinade tempers the heat from the Sriracha and keeps this dish family-friendly.

6 medium beets
4 (6-ounce) skinless, boneless chicken breast halves
1/2 cup plain 2% reduced-fat Greek yogurt
1/4 cup Sriracha (hot chile sauce)
3 tablespoons olive oil, divided
1 teaspoon freshly ground black pepper, divided
1/2 teaspoon kosher salt, divided
1/4 cup white wine vinegar
1 tablespoon honey
1 shallot, minced
6 ears shucked corn
6 cups packed fresh spinach
4 ounces goat cheese, cut into 6 slices
6 tablespoons chopped pecans, toasted

1. Leave root and 1-inch stem on beets; scrub with a brush. Place beets in a saucepan; cover with water. Bring to a boil. Reduce heat; simmer 1 hour or until tender. Drain. Cool beets slightly. Trim off beet roots and stems; rub off skins. Chop beets.
2. While beets cook, place each chicken breast half between 2 sheets of heavy-duty plastic wrap; pound to ½-inch thickness using a meat mallet or small heavy skillet. Combine yogurt and Sriracha in a heavy-duty zip-top plastic bag. Add chicken to bag; seal. Marinate in refrigerator 30 minutes, turning occasionally. Remove chicken from bag; discard marinade.
3. Preheat grill to medium-high heat.
4. Combine 2 tablespoons oil, ½ teaspoon pepper, ¼ teaspoon salt, and next 3 ingredients (through shallot) in a small bowl; stir with a whisk.
5. Place chicken on grill rack; grill 6 minutes on each side or until done. Cut chicken into 1-inch strips.
6. Brush 1 tablespoon oil over corn; sprinkle with ½ teaspoon pepper and ¼ teaspoon salt. Grill 10 minutes or until lightly charred, turning corn occasionally. Cool. Cut kernels from ears of corn.
7. Arrange 1 cup spinach on each of 6 plates; top each serving with 3 ounces chicken, ⅓ cup beets, ⅓ cup corn, 1 cheese slice, and 1 tablespoon pecans. Drizzle 1 tablespoon dressing over each salad. Yield: 6 servings.

CALORIES 456; **FAT** 21.9g (sat 6.5g, mono 10.5g, poly 3.6g); **PROTEIN** 35.1g; **CARB** 33.5g; **FIBER** 7.4g; **CHOL** 78mg; **IRON** 4.9mg; **SODIUM** 614mg; **CALC** 175mg

KID-FRIENDLY / MAKE-AHEAD / PORTABLE

CREAMY CHICKEN SALAD

Poaching the chicken keeps it moist and succulent, so you'll need less dressing to bind the salad.

2 pounds skinless, boneless chicken breast halves
1/2 cup light mayonnaise
1/2 cup plain 2% reduced-fat Greek yogurt
1 tablespoon fresh lemon juice
1 tablespoon white wine vinegar
1 tablespoon Dijon mustard
1 teaspoon honey
1/2 teaspoon kosher salt
1/2 teaspoon freshly ground black pepper
1/3 cup chopped celery
1/3 cup sweetened dried cranberries
7 tablespoons (about 2 ounces) coarsely chopped smoked almonds
6 cups mixed salad greens

1. Fill a Dutch oven two-thirds full of water; bring to a boil.

2. Wrap each chicken breast half completely and tightly in heavy-duty plastic wrap. Add chicken to boiling water. Cover and simmer 20 minutes or until a thermometer registers 165°. Remove from pan, and let stand 5 minutes. Unwrap chicken and shred; refrigerate 30 minutes or until cold.

3. Combine mayonnaise and next 7 ingredients (through black pepper) in a large bowl, stirring with a whisk until combined. Add chicken, 1/3 cup celery, cranberries, and almonds; toss well to coat. Cover and refrigerate 1 hour. Serve over salad greens. Yield: 6 servings (serving size: about 1 cup chicken salad and 1 cup salad greens).

CALORIES 339; **FAT** 13.6g (sat 1.9g, mono 5.1g, poly 5.1g); **PROTEIN** 39.5g; **CARB** 14.6g; **FIBER** 2.8g; **CHOL** 95mg; **IRON** 2mg; **SODIUM** 525mg; **CALC** 54mg

SUPERFAST

GRILLED CHICKEN CAESAR SALAD

This salad dressing mimics the flavor of a typical Caesar but in a vinaigrette form.

2 ounces French bread, cut into ½-inch cubes (about 2 cups)
Cooking spray
2 (8-ounce) skinless, boneless chicken breast halves, halved lengthwise
½ teaspoon black pepper, divided
2 tablespoons white wine vinegar
2 tablespoons olive oil
1 teaspoon minced garlic
1 teaspoon Dijon mustard
½ teaspoon anchovy paste
6 cups chopped romaine lettuce
2 cups chopped radicchio lettuce
¼ cup (1 ounce) grated fresh Parmesan cheese

1. Preheat oven to 400°.
2. Spread bread cubes in a single layer on a baking sheet. Bake at 400° for 9 minutes or until lightly toasted.
3. Heat a grill pan over high heat. Coat pan with cooking spray. Sprinkle chicken with ¼ teaspoon pepper. Add chicken to pan, and cook 3½ minutes on each side or until done. Remove from pan; let stand 5 minutes. Cut chicken into slices.
4. Combine ¼ teaspoon pepper, vinegar, and next 4 ingredients (through anchovy paste) in a large bowl, stirring with a whisk. Add romaine and radicchio to bowl; toss well to coat. Arrange lettuce and chicken evenly on 4 plates. Top each serving with ½ cup croutons and 1 tablespoon cheese. Yield: 4 servings.

CALORIES 272; **FAT** 10.4g (sat 2.3g, mono 5.7g, poly 1.3g); **PROTEIN** 31.1g; **CARB** 12.6g; **FIBER** 2.1g; **CHOL** 72mg; **IRON** 2.2mg; **SODIUM** 322mg; **CALC** 104mg

ANCHOVIES

Don't hold the anchovy! A little anchovy or anchovy paste (a mixture of pounded anchovies, vinegar, and salt) adds savory depth to dressings. Anchovies contain vitamin D and omega-3 fatty acids, and they are also low in mercury and other contaminants.

MAKE-AHEAD / SUPERFAST

GRILLED CHICKEN AND SPINACH SALAD WITH SPICY PINEAPPLE DRESSING

The sweetness of pineapple and orange juice both complement and balance the spicy ingredients in this salad. Be sure to wear gloves when working with habanero peppers.

1 pound skinless, boneless chicken breast
1 teaspoon chili powder
1/2 teaspoon salt
Cooking spray
1 1/4 cups (1-inch) cubed fresh pineapple (about 8 ounces), divided
2 tablespoons chopped fresh cilantro
2 tablespoons fresh orange juice
4 teaspoons apple cider vinegar
1/2 teaspoon minced habanero pepper
1 large garlic clove
1/4 cup extra-virgin olive oil
3/4 cup julienne-cut peeled jicama
2/3 cup thinly sliced red bell pepper
1/2 cup thinly sliced red onion
1 (5-ounce) package fresh baby spinach (about 8 cups)

1. Heat a grill pan over medium-high heat. Place chicken between 2 sheets of plastic wrap, and pound to an even thickness using a meat mallet or small heavy skillet. Sprinkle both sides of chicken evenly with chili powder and salt. Lightly coat chicken with cooking spray. Add chicken to pan; cook 3 minutes on each side or until done. Remove from pan; set aside.

2. Place half of pineapple and next 5 ingredients (through garlic) in a blender; process until smooth. With blender on, gradually add olive oil until blended.

3. Combine remaining pineapple, jicama, and next 3 ingredients (through spinach) in a large bowl. Drizzle with 3/4 cup dressing, and toss gently to coat. Arrange salad evenly on each of 4 plates. Cut chicken across grain into thin slices; divide chicken evenly over salads. Drizzle salads evenly with 1/4 cup dressing. Yield: 4 servings.

CALORIES 313; **FAT** 15.2g (sat 2.3g, mono 10.2g, poly 1.8g); **PROTEIN** 28g; **CARB** 16.8g; **FIBER** 4.3g; **CHOL** 66mg; **IRON** 2.6mg; **SODIUM** 444mg; **CALC** 58mg

JICAMA

An edible root that resembles a turnip, jicama (HEE-kah-ma) has thin brown skin and crisp, juicy, white flesh that's mild in flavor—think of a cross between a water chestnut and a pear. Choose firm roots with dry, unblemished skin.

SUPERFAST

ROAST CHICKEN SALAD WITH PEACHES, GOAT CHEESE, AND PECANS

Fresh peaches and goat cheese headline this simple, no-cook salad recipe. The eight-ingredient vinaigrette, made with pantry staples, takes minutes to make and is a delicious complement to the other ingredients in the salad. Use a store-bought rotisserie chicken to save time in the kitchen. Serve with herbed bread.

2½ tablespoons balsamic vinegar
1½ tablespoons extra-virgin olive oil
1½ tablespoons minced shallots
2½ teaspoons fresh lemon juice
2½ teaspoons maple syrup
¾ teaspoon Dijon mustard
¼ teaspoon kosher salt
¼ teaspoon freshly ground black pepper
2 cups shredded skinless, boneless rotisserie chicken breast
2 cups sliced peeled peaches
½ cup vertically sliced red onion
¼ cup chopped pecans, toasted
1 (5-ounce) package gourmet salad greens
2 tablespoons crumbled goat cheese

1. Combine first 8 ingredients; stir with a whisk.
2. Combine chicken and next 4 ingredients (through greens) in a large bowl. Add vinaigrette mixture; toss gently. Sprinkle with cheese. Yield: 4 servings (serving size: about 1¾ cups salad and 1½ teaspoons cheese).

CALORIES 285; **FAT** 14g (sat 2.4g, mono 7.8g, poly 2.8g); **PROTEIN** 24.6g; **CARB** 16g; **FIBER** 2.9g; **CHOL** 61mg; **IRON** 1.9mg; **SODIUM** 203mg; **CALC** 54mg

100-CALORIE SALAD BOOSTERS

Start with 1½ cups of fresh mixed greens. Add a tablespoon of your favorite vinaigrette. Then pile on the good stuff. Give your salad some south-of-the-border inspiration with this flavor combination.

2 TABLESPOONS RINSED AND DRAINED BLACK BEANS

2 TABLESPOONS CRUMBLED QUESO FRESCO

2 TABLESPOONS CUBED AVOCADO

2 TABLESPOONS SWEET YELLOW CORN

SUPERFAST

SOUTHWESTERN COBB SALAD

This version of a Cobb salad combines south-of-the-border flavors with the turkey and bacon that are traditional in a Cobb.

Vinaigrette:

3 tablespoons white wine vinegar
1 teaspoon honey
3/4 teaspoon ground cumin
1/2 teaspoon smoked paprika
1/2 teaspoon garlic powder
1/4 teaspoon ground red pepper
2 tablespoons canola oil

Salad:

3 center-cut bacon slices
Cooking spray
8 ounces skinless, boneless turkey breast, cut into 1/2-inch pieces
1/4 teaspoon salt
8 cups torn romaine lettuce
1/2 cup refrigerated fresh pico de gallo
1/2 cup diced avocado
1/2 cup (2 ounces) crumbled queso fresco
1/4 cup chopped green onions
1 (15-ounce) can low-sodium black beans, rinsed and drained

1. To prepare vinaigrette, combine first 6 ingredients in a medium bowl, stirring with a whisk. Gradually add oil, stirring constantly with a whisk; set aside.

2. To prepare salad, cook bacon in a nonstick skillet over medium heat until crisp. Remove bacon from pan; crumble. Wipe pan clean with paper towels. Increase heat to medium-high. Coat pan with cooking spray. Sprinkle turkey with salt. Add turkey to pan; sauté 4 minutes or until done.

3. Arrange 2 cups lettuce on each of 4 plates. Top each serving with about 2 teaspoons bacon, 5 tablespoons turkey, 2 tablespoons pico de gallo, 2 tablespoons avocado, 2 tablespoons queso fresco, 1 tablespoon onions, and about ⅓ cup beans. Drizzle vinaigrette evenly over salads. Yield: 4 servings.

CALORIES 293; **FAT** 13.6g (sat 2.5g, mono 7.2g, poly 3g); **PROTEIN** 22.4g; **CARB** 19.9g; **FIBER** 6.6g; **CHOL** 44mg; **IRON** 3.1mg; **SODIUM** 455mg; **CALC** 117mg

TERIYAKI MUSHROOM, SPINACH, AND CHICKEN SALAD

You can use up any leftover cooked chicken in your fridge: Simply skip the first step, and cut or shred precooked chicken into pieces.

2 tablespoons peanut oil, divided
8 ounces skinless, boneless chicken breast, cut into small pieces
1/2 teaspoon freshly ground black pepper, divided
1/4 teaspoon salt, divided
10 cups sliced shiitake mushroom caps (about 1 pound)
2 tablespoons minced peeled fresh ginger
1 tablespoon minced garlic
3 tablespoons lower-sodium soy sauce
3 tablespoons mirin (sweet rice wine) or 2 tablespoons water plus 1 tablespoon honey
1 teaspoon rice vinegar
8 cups baby spinach leaves (about 6 ounces)
1 3/4 cups chopped green onions

1. Heat a large skillet over high heat. Add 1 tablespoon oil to pan; swirl to coat. Add chicken; sprinkle with ¼ teaspoon pepper and ⅛ teaspoon salt. Cook 3 minutes or until chicken is just done, stirring occasionally. Remove chicken from pan.

2. Add mushrooms, ¼ teaspoon pepper, and ⅛ teaspoon salt to pan; stir-fry 6 minutes or until mushrooms brown and most of liquid evaporates. Add 1 tablespoon oil, ginger, and garlic to pan; cook 30 seconds, stirring constantly. Return chicken to pan; add soy sauce, mirin, and vinegar to pan. Cook 2 minutes, scraping pan to loosen browned bits. Remove pan from heat; stir in spinach and onions. Yield: 4 servings (serving size: 1½ cups).

CALORIES 205; **FAT** 8.4g (sat 1.5g, mono 3.6g, poly 2.8g); **PROTEIN** 19.3g; **CARB** 13.4g; **FIBER** 3.1g; **CHOL** 33mg; **IRON** 2.9mg; **SODIUM** 629mg; **CALC** 82mg

KID-FRIENDLY / SUPERFAST

THAI CHICKEN SALAD WITH PEANUT DRESSING

Consider this a tropical version of a creamy chicken salad: The dressing is a warm, decadent mix of coconut milk and peanut butter.

6 cups torn romaine lettuce
2 cups shredded skinless, boneless rotisserie chicken breast
2 cups fresh bean sprouts
1 cup shredded carrot
3/4 cup sliced celery
2/3 cup light coconut milk
1 tablespoon brown sugar
2 tablespoons creamy peanut butter
1 tablespoon fresh lime juice
2 tablespoons lower-sodium soy sauce
1/8 teaspoon ground red pepper
2 tablespoons coarsely chopped unsalted, dry-roasted peanuts
4 lime wedges (optional)

1. Combine first 5 ingredients in a large bowl.
2. Combine coconut milk and next 5 ingredients (through red pepper) in a small saucepan; bring to a boil. Reduce heat, and simmer 5 minutes or until mixture thickens slightly, stirring occasionally. Remove from heat, and cool 2 minutes.
3. Pour warm coconut milk mixture over lettuce mixture. Sprinkle with peanuts; serve with lime wedges, if desired. Serve immediately. Yield: 4 servings (serving size: 3 cups salad and 1½ teaspoons peanuts).

CALORIES 262; **FAT** 11.2g (sat 3.7g, mono 4.5g, poly 2.5g); **PROTEIN** 27.5g; **CARB** 17.1g; **FIBER** 4.4g; **CHOL** 63mg; **IRON** 2.3mg; **SODIUM** 599mg; **CALC** 67mg

COCONUT MILK

Coconut milk, the "cream" of the tropics, is a result of blending freshly grated coconut with hot water and then straining. The ratio of coconut to water can be changed to make a richer or lighter milk, and coconut can be used several times to make coconut milk, though the results will be lighter each time.

KID-FRIENDLY / MAKE-AHEAD / PORTABLE

CHICKEN TABBOULEH WITH TAHINI DRIZZLE

One sure sign that the bulgur is done—little holes form on top.

1¼ cups water
1 cup uncooked bulgur, rinsed and drained
2 tablespoons olive oil, divided
1 teaspoon kosher salt, divided
½ pound skinless, boneless chicken thighs
½ teaspoon freshly ground black pepper
3 cups chopped tomato
1 cup chopped fresh parsley
1 cup chopped fresh mint
1 cup chopped green onions
1 teaspoon minced garlic
¼ cup tahini (roasted sesame seed paste)
¼ cup plain 2% reduced-fat Greek yogurt
3 tablespoons fresh lemon juice
1 tablespoon water

1. Combine 1¼ cups water, 1 cup bulgur, 1 tablespoon olive oil, and ½ teaspoon salt in a medium saucepan; bring to a boil. Reduce heat; simmer 10 minutes (do not stir) or until liquid almost evaporates. Remove from heat; fluff with a fork. Place bulgur in a medium bowl; let stand 10 minutes.
2. Heat 1 tablespoon oil in a large nonstick skillet over medium-high heat. Add chicken to pan; sprinkle with ¼ teaspoon salt and black pepper. Sauté 4 minutes on each side or until done; shred chicken. Combine bulgur, chicken, tomato, and next 4 ingredients (through garlic) in a large bowl; toss gently.
3. Combine ¼ teaspoon salt, tahini, and next 3 ingredients (through water) in a small bowl, stirring with a whisk. Drizzle over salad. Yield: 4 servings (serving size: about 1½ cups).

CALORIES 295; **FAT** 18.2g (sat 3g, mono 8.8g, poly 5.1g); **PROTEIN** 21.5g; **CARB** 41g; **FIBER** 10.9g; **CHOL** 48mg; **IRON** 4.2mg; **SODIUM** 573mg; **CALC** 127mg

KID-FRIENDLY / SUPERFAST

TURKEY AND ROMAINE SALAD ➤

¼ cup low-fat buttermilk (1%)
1 tablespoon light mayonnaise
1 tablespoon fresh lime juice
⅛ teaspoon salt
⅛ teaspoon ground red pepper
1 garlic clove, peeled
½ ripe peeled avocado, seeded and coarsely mashed
8 (½-ounce) slices diagonally cut French bread baguette (about ½ inch thick)
¼ cup (1 ounce) preshredded Parmesan cheese
4 cups bagged chopped romaine lettuce
1½ cups diced deli, lower-salt turkey breast (about 6 ounces)
½ cup thinly sliced green onions
2 tablespoons chopped fresh cilantro

1. Place first 7 ingredients in a blender, and process until smooth, scraping sides. Set aside.
2. Preheat broiler.
3. Arrange bread slices in a single layer on a baking sheet. Sprinkle 1½ teaspoons cheese on each bread slice. Broil bread slices 2 minutes or until lightly browned.
4. Combine lettuce and next 3 ingredients (through cilantro) in a large bowl. Drizzle buttermilk mixture over lettuce mixture; toss gently to coat. Serve with cheese toasts. Yield: 4 servings (serving size: about 1½ cups salad and 2 cheese toasts).

CALORIES 235; **FAT** 8.3g (sat 2.3g, mono 3.3g, poly 0.9g); **PROTEIN** 17g; **CARB** 22.7g; **FIBER** 3.9g; **CHOL** 24mg; **IRON** 2.2mg; **SODIUM** 640mg; **CALC** 144mg

KID-FRIENDLY

PORK AND NOODLE SALAD

Pork cooks quickly in the broiler, making this meal a clear choice for busy weeknight dinners.

6 ounces uncooked rice vermicelli
1/4 cup rice vinegar
1 tablespoon sugar
3 tablespoons mirin (sweet rice wine)
2 tablespoons water
2 teaspoons fish sauce
1 cup julienne-cut carrot
3/4 cup thinly sliced red bell pepper (about 1 small pepper)
1/2 cup thinly sliced green onions
1/3 cup thinly sliced fresh basil
1/4 cup chopped dry-roasted peanuts
2 tablespoons hoisin sauce
1 teaspoon rice vinegar
1 teaspoon bottled ground fresh ginger
1/2 teaspoon minced garlic
4 (4-ounce) boneless center-cut pork loin chops
1/4 teaspoon salt
1/8 teaspoon freshly ground black pepper
Cooking spray

1. Preheat broiler.
2. Cook noodles according to package directions. Drain and rinse under cold water; drain. Place noodles in a large bowl. Add 1/4 cup vinegar and next 4 ingredients (through fish sauce); toss well. Top with carrot, bell pepper, green onions, basil, and peanuts.
3. Combine hoisin and next 3 ingredients (through garlic). Sprinkle pork evenly with salt and black pepper; place on a broiler pan coated with cooking spray. Brush half of hoisin mixture over pork; broil 3 minutes. Turn pork over. Brush remaining hoisin mixture over pork; broil 3 minutes or until done. Thinly slice pork. Serve pork over salad. Yield: 4 servings (serving size: about 1¾ cups salad and 1 pork chop).

CALORIES 441; **FAT** 12.5g (sat 2.4g, mono 4.3g, poly 2.3g); **PROTEIN** 24.8g; **CARB** 50.2g; **FIBER** 3.2g; **CHOL** 58mg; **IRON** 2.4mg; **SODIUM** 596mg; **CALC** 81mg

MIRIN

Made from rice, this sweet cooking wine lends sweetness to round out the saltiness of some dishes and subdue the fishiness of others. You can find mirin at specialty grocery stores or at Asian markets.

PORK, PINEAPPLE, AND ANAHEIM CHILE SALAD WITH AVOCADO

Pork has a natural affinity for fruit, and grilling the pineapple intensifies its sweet flavor.

Pork:

3/4 teaspoon ground coriander
3/4 teaspoon ground cumin
1/2 teaspoon kosher salt
1/2 teaspoon freshly ground black pepper
1 (1-pound) pork tenderloin, trimmed
1 tablespoon olive oil
Cooking spray

Vinaigrette:

1 1/2 tablespoons chopped fresh cilantro
1 1/2 tablespoons fresh lime juice
1 tablespoon olive oil
1 tablespoon water
1/2 teaspoon kosher salt
1/2 teaspoon sugar
1/2 teaspoon freshly ground black pepper
1 garlic clove, minced

Salad:

1/2 fresh pineapple, peeled, cored, and cut into (1/2-inch-thick) rings
2 Anaheim chiles
1 red bell pepper, seeded and halved
12 Boston lettuce leaves
3/4 cup cubed avocado

1. Preheat grill to medium-high heat.

2. To prepare pork, combine first 4 ingredients. Brush pork with 1 tablespoon oil; rub spice mixture over pork.

3. Place pork on grill rack coated with cooking spray, and grill 20 minutes or until thermometer registers 155° (slightly pink), turning pork occasionally. Transfer to a cutting board, and let rest 10 minutes. Cut pork crosswise into thin slices.

4. To prepare vinaigrette, combine cilantro and next 7 ingredients (through garlic) in a bowl, stirring well with a whisk.

5. To prepare salad, place pineapple, chiles, and bell pepper halves, skin sides down, on grill rack lightly coated with cooking spray; grill 5 minutes. Turn pineapple and chiles; grill 5 minutes. Place bell pepper and chiles in a zip-top plastic bag; seal. Let stand 10 minutes. Remove pepper and chiles from bag. Seed chiles. Peel pepper and chiles, and finely chop. Chop pineapple. Place pepper, chiles, and pineapple in a bowl. Drizzle with vinaigrette; toss. Arrange 2 lettuce leaves on each of 6 plates. Divide pork evenly among salads. Spoon ½ cup pineapple mixture over each serving, and sprinkle each serving with 2 tablespoons avocado. Serve immediately. Yield: 6 servings.

CALORIES 235; **FAT** 11.8g (sat 2.2g, mono 7.2g, poly 1.3g); **PROTEIN** 17.1g; **CARB** 17.3g; **FIBER** 4.7g; **CHOL** 42mg; **IRON** 2.1mg; **SODIUM** 363mg; **CALC** 41mg

KID-FRIENDLY

PORK TENDERLOIN, PEAR, AND CRANBERRY SALAD

Enjoy fall flavors with this salad. The sweetness of the pear and the tang from the cranberries and cranberry juice complement each other nicely.

1 tablespoon cider vinegar
1 teaspoon Dijon mustard
3/4 teaspoon brown sugar
1 1/2 teaspoons minced fresh garlic, divided
1 1/4 teaspoons dried thyme, divided
1 pound pork tenderloin, trimmed and cut crosswise into 1/4-inch-thick slices
3/4 teaspoon salt, divided
3/4 teaspoon freshly ground black pepper, divided
2 tablespoons all-purpose flour
1/4 cup olive oil, divided
1/4 cup sliced shallots
1/4 cup dried cranberries
1/4 cup cranberry juice cocktail
6 cups baby spinach leaves
1 ripe red Anjou pear, thinly sliced

1. Combine vinegar, mustard, sugar, ½ teaspoon garlic, and ¼ teaspoon thyme; set aside.
2. Combine pork, 1 teaspoon garlic, 1 teaspoon thyme, ½ teaspoon salt, and ½ teaspoon pepper; toss well to coat. Sprinkle pork mixture with flour; toss well. Let stand 5 minutes.
3. Heat 1 tablespoon oil in a medium saucepan over medium heat. Add shallots to pan; cook 3 minutes or until shallots are tender and lightly browned, stirring occasionally. Add cranberries and juice to pan; cook until liquid is reduced to 2 tablespoons (about 2 minutes). Reduce heat to medium-low. Add vinegar mixture to pan; cook 1 minute. Gradually add 1 tablespoon oil, ¼ teaspoon salt, and ¼ teaspoon black pepper, stirring well with a whisk. Cover and keep warm.
4. Heat 1 tablespoon oil in a large nonstick skillet over medium-high heat. Add half of pork to skillet; cook 3 minutes or until browned, turning once. Remove pork from skillet. Repeat procedure with 1 tablespoon oil and remaining pork. Toss pork with 1 tablespoon warm cranberry mixture.
5. Combine spinach and pear in a large bowl. Drizzle with remaining cranberry mixture; toss well to coat. Arrange about 2 cups spinach mixture on each of 4 plates; top evenly with pork. Yield: 4 servings.

CALORIES 360; **FAT** 17.7g (sat 3.3g, mono 11.6g, poly 1.9g); **PROTEIN** 25.8g; **CARB** 25.6g; **FIBER** 4.4g; **CHOL** 74mg; **IRON** 3.3mg; **SODIUM** 593mg; **CALC** 71mg

KID-FRIENDLY / SUPERFAST

PROSCIUTTO, PEACH, AND SWEET LETTUCE SALAD

Serve this light main-course salad with a hunk of crusty baguette and a glass of chilled Riesling. Choose ripe, juicy peaches, and leave the peel on for more texture. Ricotta salata is a milky, mild, slightly salty cheese that's easy to crumble; you can substitute feta or goat cheese.

2 tablespoons fresh lemon juice
2 teaspoons honey
1/4 teaspoon freshly ground black pepper
1/8 teaspoon salt
2 tablespoons extra-virgin olive oil
1 tablespoon finely chopped fresh mint
1 (6.5-ounce) package sweet butter lettuce mix
2 large ripe peaches, cut into wedges
3 ounces very thin slices prosciutto, cut into 1-inch pieces
3 ounces ricotta salata, divided into pieces
2 tablespoons dry-roasted sunflower seed kernels
Small fresh mint leaves (optional)

1. Combine first 4 ingredients, stirring with a whisk. Gradually drizzle in olive oil, stirring constantly with a whisk. Stir in chopped mint.
2. Combine lettuce mix and peach wedges in a large bowl. Drizzle lettuce mixture with dressing; toss gently to coat. Place about 2 cups salad on each of 4 plates; top each serving with ¾ ounce prosciutto, ¾ ounce ricotta salata, and about 2 teaspoons sunflower seed kernels. Garnish with small mint leaves, if desired. Yield: 4 servings.

CALORIES 209; **FAT** 13.5g (sat 3.2g, mono 5.9g, poly 2.2g); **PROTEIN** 10.4g; **CARB** 14.3g; **FIBER** 2.1g; **CHOL** 26mg; **IRON** 1.4mg; **SODIUM** 530mg; **CALC** 87mg

PROSCIUTTO

Unlike American ham, prosciutto isn't smoked but rather air-dried and cured with salt and seasonings. The meat is pressed, resulting in smooth, thin slices.

SUPERFAST

SPINACH SALAD WITH SPICED PORK AND GINGER DRESSING

Crisp flatbread can round out this satisfying salad supper. You can also serve the seasoned pork as an entrée without the salad, if you wish.

1 (1-pound) pork tenderloin, trimmed
1 tablespoon Sriracha (hot chile sauce)
2 tablespoons brown sugar
1/2 teaspoon garlic powder
1/4 teaspoon salt
Cooking spray
3 cups baby spinach leaves
2 cups thinly sliced napa (Chinese) cabbage
1 cup red bell pepper strips
1/4 cup low-fat sesame ginger dressing

1. Cut pork crosswise into ½-inch slices; flatten each slice slightly with your hand. Combine pork and Sriracha in a bowl, tossing to coat. Add sugar, garlic powder, and salt; toss well.
2. Heat a large nonstick skillet over medium-high heat. Coat pan with cooking spray. Add pork mixture to pan, and cook 3 minutes on each side or until done. Remove from heat; keep warm.
3. Combine spinach, cabbage, and bell pepper in a large bowl. Add sesame ginger dressing; toss well. Arrange 1½ cups spinach mixture in each of 4 shallow bowls; top each serving with 3 ounces pork. Yield: 4 servings.

CALORIES 202; **FAT** 4.7g (sat 1.4g, mono 1.8g, poly 0.5g); **PROTEIN** 25g; **CARB** 14.7g; **FIBER** 1.9g; **CHOL** 74mg; **IRON** 2.2mg; **SODIUM** 490mg; **CALC** 56mg

MINT

Mint balances the fire in spicy dishes, making it an important herb in Middle Eastern, Asian, and Latin cuisines.

VIETNAMESE SALAD

1 (1-pound) pork tenderloin, trimmed
1 teaspoon canola oil
Cooking spray
3 tablespoons fresh lime juice
1 1/2 tablespoons fish sauce
1 1/2 tablespoons lower-sodium soy sauce
1 1/2 teaspoons sugar
1 1/2 teaspoons grated peeled fresh ginger
1/8 teaspoon ground red pepper
1 serrano chile, thinly sliced
3/4 cup small fresh mint leaves
1/2 cup thinly sliced red onion
3 thinly diagonally sliced green onions
1 cucumber, halved lengthwise, seeded, and thinly sliced
8 cups sliced romaine lettuce
1/2 cup cilantro leaves

1. Preheat grill to medium-high heat.
2. Brush pork with oil. Place pork on grill rack coated with cooking spray; grill 6 minutes on each side or until a thermometer inserted into thickest portion of pork registers 145°. Remove from grill; let pork stand 5 minutes. Slice pork crosswise in half; slice each half, lengthwise, into thin strips. Cool.
3. Combine juice and next 6 ingredients (through serrano) in a large bowl. Add pork to juice mixture; toss to coat. Add mint and next 3 ingredients (through cucumber) to bowl; toss. Arrange 2 cups lettuce on each of 4 plates; top each serving with about ⅔ cup pork mixture. Sprinkle evenly with cilantro. Yield: 4 servings.

CALORIES 200; **FAT** 4.3g (sat 1g, mono 1.7g, poly 1g); **PROTEIN** 27.7g; **CARB** 13.9g; **FIBER** 5g; **CHOL** 74mg; **IRON** 3.4mg; **SODIUM** 653mg; **CALC** 95mg

SUPERFAST

WARM SPINACH SALAD WITH PORK AND PEARS

Serve a loaf of whole-grain or sesame seed bread to complete the dinner. Blue cheese balances the sweetness of the pears and raisins.

Cooking spray
1 (1-pound) pork tenderloin, trimmed and cut crosswise into 12 slices
½ teaspoon salt, divided
¼ teaspoon freshly ground black pepper, divided
3 tablespoons water
3 tablespoons sherry vinegar or red wine vinegar
1 tablespoon extra-virgin olive oil
2 cups thinly sliced Anjou or Bartlett pear (about 2)
¼ cup golden raisins
1 (5-ounce) package fresh baby spinach
2 tablespoons crumbled blue cheese

1. Heat a large nonstick skillet over medium-high heat. Coat pan with cooking spray. Sprinkle pork evenly with ¼ teaspoon salt and ⅛ teaspoon pepper. Add pork to pan; cook 4 minutes on each side or until browned.
2. Combine ¼ teaspoon salt, ⅛ teaspoon pepper, 3 tablespoons water, vinegar, and oil in a small bowl, stirring with a whisk.
3. Combine pear, raisins, and spinach in a large bowl; toss well. Arrange 2 cups spinach mixture on each of 4 plates, and drizzle evenly with vinegar mixture. Top each serving with 3 pork slices and 1½ teaspoons cheese. Yield: 4 servings.

CALORIES 296; **FAT** 10.1g (sat 3g, mono 4.8g, poly 0.8g); **PROTEIN** 25.5g; **CARB** 27.4g; **FIBER** 4.5g; **CHOL** 68mg; **IRON** 2.8mg; **SODIUM** 471mg; **CALC** 117mg

PEARS

Choose pears with stems attached and unblemished, unbroken skin. Press gently on the stem ends to check for ripeness. If the pears are firm, you can easily ripen them at home; just store them at room temperature.

SUPERFAST

BARBECUE SIRLOIN AND BLUE CHEESE SALAD

Lean sirloin steak sits atop a bed of fresh veggies for an easy weeknight main-dish salad. Top with crumbles of rich blue cheese to bring out the bold flavors in the homemade vinaigrette.

2 teaspoons chili powder
3/4 teaspoon ground cumin
1/2 teaspoon garlic powder
1/4 teaspoon salt
1/4 teaspoon freshly ground black pepper, divided
1 pound lean sirloin steak, trimmed
Cooking spray
2 tablespoons white wine vinegar
2 teaspoons Dijon mustard
1 tablespoon extra-virgin olive oil
6 cups torn Bibb lettuce
3/4 cup thinly sliced peeled cucumber
1 cup red bell pepper strips
1/2 cup thinly sliced shallots
1/2 cup (2 ounces) crumbled blue cheese

1. Combine chili powder, cumin, garlic powder, ¼ teaspoon salt, and ⅛ teaspoon black pepper; rub evenly over both sides of steak.

2. Heat a grill pan over medium-high heat. Coat pan with cooking spray. Add steak to pan; cook 5 minutes. Turn steak over; cook 4 minutes or until desired degree of doneness. Place steak on a cutting board; let stand 5 minutes. Cut across grain into thin slices.

3. Combine vinegar, mustard, and ⅛ teaspoon black pepper in a small bowl, stirring with a whisk. Gradually add oil, stirring with a whisk. Combine lettuce, cucumber, bell pepper, and shallots in a large bowl. Drizzle vinaigrette over salad; toss gently to coat. Arrange 1½ cups salad on each of 4 plates. Top each with 3 ounces steak and 2 tablespoons cheese. Yield: 4 servings.

CALORIES 269; **FAT** 12.4g (sat 4.9g, mono 5.4g, poly 0.8g); **PROTEIN** 29.5g; **CARB** 9.4g; **FIBER** 2.6g; **CHOL** 57mg; **IRON** 2.8mg; **SODIUM** 524mg; **CALC** 141mg

MAKE-AHEAD

COLD BEEF AND NOODLE SALAD

Substitute top sirloin, strip steak, or flank steak if tri-tip steak isn't available, and slice thinly instead of into cubes.

1 (1½-pound) tri-tip steak, trimmed
¼ teaspoon kosher salt
¾ teaspoon freshly ground black pepper
2 tablespoons sherry vinegar, divided
1½ tablespoons hoisin sauce, divided
Cooking spray
8 ounces uncooked udon noodles (thick, round fresh Japanese wheat noodles) or spaghetti
2 tablespoons chopped fresh cilantro
3½ tablespoons lower-sodium soy sauce
3 tablespoons canola oil
1 tablespoon fresh lime juice
1 teaspoon crushed red pepper
¾ teaspoon grated peeled fresh ginger
½ cup thinly sliced green onions
3 garlic cloves, minced
2 cups (3-inch) julienne-cut baby bok choy (about 6 ounces)
½ cup thinly sliced shiitake mushroom caps (about 2 ounces)
½ cup thinly sliced radishes
½ cup thinly sliced shallots
¼ cup thinly sliced fresh mint
Lime wedges (optional)
Sriracha (hot chile sauce) (optional)

1. Preheat grill to high heat.
2. Sprinkle steak with salt and black pepper. Combine 1 tablespoon vinegar and 1 tablespoon hoisin in a small bowl; stir with a whisk. Place steak on grill rack coated with cooking spray. Brush steak with hoisin mixture; grill 10 minutes. Turn steak. Brush with hoisin mixture; grill 10 minutes or until desired degree of doneness. Remove from heat; chill 45 minutes. Cut steak into ½-inch cubes.
3. Cook noodles according to package directions, omitting salt and fat; drain well.
4. Combine 1 tablespoon vinegar, 1½ teaspoons hoisin, cilantro, and next 7 ingredients (through garlic) in a large bowl; stir with a whisk. Add beef, noodles, bok choy, and mushrooms; toss to combine. Chill 15 minutes; top with radishes, shallots, and mint. Serve with lime wedges and Sriracha, if desired. Yield: 6 servings (serving size: about 1½ cups).

CALORIES 402; **FAT** 14.8g (sat 2.5g, mono 7.3g, poly 2.4g); **PROTEIN** 31.7g; **CARB** 33.7g; **FIBER** 3.2g; **CHOL** 49mg; **IRON** 3.9mg; **SODIUM** 515mg; **CALC** 89mg

MAKE-AHEAD / SUPERFAST

FIERY BEEF AND RICE NOODLE SALAD

Think salads aren't filling? Then you haven't tried this one packed with rice noodles, fresh vegetables, and tender steak.

2 ounces uncooked rice sticks (rice-flour noodles)
12 ounces flank steak, trimmed
¼ teaspoon salt
¼ teaspoon freshly ground black pepper
Cooking spray
2 cups shredded iceberg lettuce
⅓ cup thinly vertically sliced red onion
1 cucumber, peeled, halved lengthwise, and thinly sliced
½ habanero pepper, minced
¼ cup fresh lime juice
1 tablespoon sugar
1 tablespoon fish sauce
12 fresh basil leaves, torn

1. Cook noodles according to package directions. Drain and rinse with cold water; drain. Coarsely chop noodles.

2. While noodles cook, freeze steak 5 minutes. Remove from freezer; cut across grain into ⅛-inch-thick slices. Sprinkle with salt and black pepper.

3. Heat a large cast-iron skillet over medium-high heat. Coat with cooking spray. Add beef; sauté 4 minutes.

4. Combine steak, noodles, lettuce, onion, cucumber, and habanero. Combine juice, sugar, and fish sauce; pour over noodle mixture, tossing gently. Sprinkle with basil.

Yield: 4 servings (serving size: 1½ cups salad and about 1 tablespoon basil).

CALORIES 197; **FAT** 4.3g (sat 1.7g, mono 1.6g, poly 0.2g); **PROTEIN** 20g; **CARB** 20.2g; **FIBER** 1.3g; **CHOL** 27mg; **IRON** 1.8mg; **SODIUM** 545mg; **CALC** 35mg

Habaneros are small, but they pack a lot of punch. They have a distinct sweetness and intensely hot spice. Also available when green and red, they are ripe—and at their hottest—when orange.

SUPERFAST

FLANK STEAK SALAD WITH PLUMS AND BLUE CHEESE

Combine the comforting flavors of steak and cheese with fresh summer greens and fruit for a filling salad that's less than 300 calories per serving.

½ teaspoon freshly ground black pepper
⅜ teaspoon salt, divided
1½ tablespoons olive oil, divided
4 teaspoons fresh lemon juice, divided
1 (1-pound) flank steak, trimmed
Cooking spray
1 teaspoon honey
8 cups loosely packed baby arugula
3 plums, thinly sliced
¼ cup (1 ounce) crumbled blue cheese

1. Combine pepper, ¼ teaspoon salt, 1½ teaspoons olive oil, and 1 teaspoon lemon juice in a small bowl; rub over both sides of steak.
2. Heat a large skillet over medium-high heat. Coat pan with cooking spray. Add steak to pan; cook 5 minutes on each side or until desired degree of doneness. Remove steak from pan; let rest 5 minutes. Cut steak diagonally across grain into thin slices.
3. Combine 1 tablespoon olive oil, 1 tablespoon lemon juice, honey, and ⅛ teaspoon salt in a large bowl; stir well with a whisk. Add arugula; toss gently to coat. Arrange about 1½ cups arugula mixture on each of 4 plates; top each serving with 3 ounces steak, about ½ cup plums, and 1 tablespoon cheese. Yield: 4 servings.

CALORIES 290; **FAT** 15.8g (sat 5.4g, mono 7.7g, poly 1.3g); **PROTEIN** 26.1g; **CARB** 11.3g; **FIBER** 1.5g; **CHOL** 48mg; **IRON** 2.1mg; **SODIUM** 373mg; **CALC** 102mg

GINGER BEEF SALAD WITH MISO VINAIGRETTE

Skip the grated cheese and croutons—an Asian-inspired salad with a homemade seven-ingredient vinaigrette makes mealtime "international." Serve with soba noodles.

Steak:

1 (1-pound) flank steak, trimmed
2 tablespoons minced peeled fresh ginger
1/8 teaspoon salt
2 garlic cloves, minced
Cooking spray

Vinaigrette:

2 tablespoons chopped fresh cilantro
2 tablespoons white miso (soybean paste)
2 tablespoons water
2 tablespoons rice vinegar
1 tablespoon canola oil
2 teaspoons grated peeled fresh ginger
1/2 teaspoon sambal oelek (ground fresh chile paste)

Salad:

6 cups torn Bibb lettuce (about 3 small heads)
3/4 cup thinly sliced yellow bell pepper
1/4 cup thinly sliced red onion
1/2 English cucumber, halved lengthwise and sliced

1. Preheat broiler.
2. To prepare steak, sprinkle steak evenly with ginger, salt, and garlic. Place on a broiler pan coated with cooking spray; broil 6 minutes on each side or until desired degree of doneness. Let stand 5 minutes. Cut steak diagonally across grain into thin slices.
3. To prepare vinaigrette, combine cilantro and next 6 ingredients (through sambal oelek) in a small bowl, stirring with a whisk. Combine lettuce and next 3 ingredients (through cucumber) in a large bowl. Drizzle half of miso mixture over lettuce mixture; toss to coat.
4. Arrange 1½ cups lettuce mixture on each of 4 plates. Top each serving with 3 ounces steak; drizzle with miso mixture. Yield: 4 servings.

CALORIES 237; **FAT** 10.1g (sat 2.7g, mono 4.4g, poly 1.3g); **PROTEIN** 27.8g; **CARB** 9.5g; **FIBER** 3g; **CHOL** 37mg; **IRON** 3.6mg; **SODIUM** 427mg; **CALC** 70mg

MISO

This fermented soybean paste originated in ancient China. Use light miso for dressings and soups. It keeps indefinitely, refrigerated in a glass jar.

KID-FRIENDLY / SUPERFAST

GRILLED STEAK WITH BABY ARUGULA AND PARMESAN SALAD

Flat-iron steaks come from the top blade portion of the chuck or shoulder section.

1 teaspoon chopped fresh thyme
3/8 teaspoon kosher salt, divided
1/2 teaspoon freshly ground black pepper, divided
4 (4-ounce) flat-iron steaks
2 lemons, halved
1 tablespoon chopped fresh chives
1 tablespoon extra-virgin olive oil
1 tablespoon lemon juice
1/2 teaspoon Dijon mustard
4 cups loosely packed baby arugula
1/4 cup (1 ounce) shaved fresh Parmigiano-Reggiano cheese

1. Heat a grill pan over medium-high heat. Combine thyme, ¼ teaspoon salt, and ¼ teaspoon pepper in a small bowl; rub evenly over steaks. Add steaks to pan; cook 4 minutes on each side or until desired degree of doneness. Remove steaks from pan. Add lemon halves, cut sides down, to pan; cook 3 minutes. Cut steaks across grain into thin slices.

2. Combine ⅛ teaspoon salt, ¼ teaspoon pepper, chives, olive oil, juice, and Dijon, and stir with a whisk. Drizzle over arugula; toss to coat. Arrange 1 steak, 1 cup arugula, and 1 lemon half on each of 4 plates; top each salad with 1 tablespoon cheese. Yield: 4 servings.

CALORIES 255; **FAT** 16.2g (sat 6g, mono 7.5g, poly 0.9g); **PROTEIN** 24.4g; **CARB** 2g; **FIBER** 0.5g; **CHOL** 75mg; **IRON** 2.9mg; **SODIUM** 376mg; **CALC** 124mg

SPICY BEEF AND TOFU SALAD

The dressing serves double-duty: Use some of it to deglaze the pan after you cook the tofu and beef so you can add those caramelized, meaty flavors to the salad.

8 ounces firm tofu, cubed
6 cups torn or chopped romaine lettuce
½ cup torn fresh mint leaves
½ cup torn fresh basil leaves
1 large cucumber, peeled, halved lengthwise, seeded, and thinly sliced
1 small red onion, thinly sliced
¼ cup fresh lime juice
1 tablespoon Thai fish sauce
2 teaspoons dark sesame oil
½ teaspoon sugar
1 serrano pepper, minced
1 tablespoon peanut oil
4 ounces skirt steak, trimmed, cut into 3 equal pieces, and cut across grain into thin strips
¼ teaspoon salt
¼ teaspoon freshly ground black pepper

1. Arrange tofu on several layers of paper towels; cover with additional paper towels. Let stand 30 minutes, pressing down occasionally.
2. Combine lettuce and next 4 ingredients (through onion) in a large bowl. Combine juice and next 4 ingredients (through serrano) in a small bowl, stirring with a whisk. Drizzle half of dressing over lettuce mixture; toss to coat.
3. Heat a large skillet over medium-high heat. Add peanut oil to pan; swirl to coat. Add tofu and beef; sprinkle with salt and black pepper. Cook 3 minutes or until tofu and meat are lightly browned, stirring once or twice. Remove pan from heat. Add remaining dressing to pan, scraping pan to loosen browned bits. Add tofu mixture to lettuce mixture; toss to combine. Yield: 4 servings (serving size: about 2¾ cups).

CALORIES 214; **FAT** 13.1g (sat 3g, mono 5.1g, poly 4.5g); **PROTEIN** 15g; **CARB** 10.8g; **FIBER** 3.2g; **CHOL** 17mg; **IRON** 2.9mg; **SODIUM** 527mg; **CALC** 105mg

FISH SAUCE

A popular condiment and ingredient in Southeast Asian cooking, fish sauce is made by fermenting small fish in brine. It is used to add both saltiness and a pungent, savory flavor to dishes (in the same way that soy sauce is used). Thai fish sauce is called nam pla; *Vietnamese fish sauce is called* nuoc nam.

fish & shellfish

Seafood, an accommodating and supportive partner to a wide range of spices and other flavorful ingredients, cooks quickly. Looking for a speedy meal? Go fish!

CHIPOTLE-RUBBED SHRIMP TACO SALAD, p. 230 →

SUPERFAST

CHIPOTLE-RUBBED SHRIMP TACO SALAD

3 tablespoons chopped fresh cilantro
3 tablespoons minced shallots
3 tablespoons fresh lime juice
2 teaspoons honey
1/8 teaspoon salt
2 tablespoons olive oil
1 refrigerated (8-inch) flour tortilla taco salad shell kit
1 pound peeled and deveined jumbo shrimp
1/2 teaspoon chili powder
1/4 teaspoon ground chipotle chile powder
1/8 teaspoon salt
Cooking spray
1 (10-ounce) package romaine salad (about 6 cups)
1 1/2 cups chopped peeled ripe mango (about 1 large)
1/2 cup cherry tomatoes, halved
4 radishes, quartered

1. Preheat oven to 350°.
2. Combine first 5 ingredients in a small bowl, stirring with a whisk. Gradually add oil, stirring constantly with a whisk.
3. Bake tortilla shells according to package directions.
4. While shells bake, heat a grill pan over medium-high heat. Combine shrimp, chili powders, and salt in a large bowl; toss well to coat. Coat pan with cooking spray. Add shrimp to pan; cook 2 minutes on each side or until done.
5. Combine lettuce, mango, tomato, and radishes. Drizzle vinaigrette over salad; toss to coat. Place about 1½ cups salad in each tortilla shell; divide shrimp evenly among salads. Yield: 4 servings (serving size: 1 salad).

CALORIES 405; **FAT** 12.5g (sat 1.8g, mono 6.8g, poly 2.4g); **PROTEIN** 29.2g; **CARB** 45.9g; **FIBER** 3.4g; **CHOL** 172mg; **IRON** 4.9mg; **SODIUM** 598mg; **CALC** 200mg

MAKE-AHEAD

CRAB SALAD-STUFFED EGGS ➤

2 cups thinly sliced radishes
1 tablespoon fresh lemon juice, divided
1/2 teaspoon salt, divided
8 large eggs
1/4 teaspoon freshly ground black pepper
2 tablespoons extra-virgin olive oil
3 tablespoons plain fat-free Greek yogurt
1 cup lump crabmeat, drained and shell pieces removed (about 5 ounces)
1/4 cup finely chopped celery
1 teaspoon dry mustard
24 butter lettuce leaves

1. Combine radishes, 2 teaspoons juice, and ¼ teaspoon salt in a bowl; toss. Cover and chill at least 30 minutes.
2. Place eggs in a medium saucepan, and cover with cold water to 1 inch above eggs; bring to a boil. Reduce heat; simmer 10 minutes. Place eggs in ice water; cool completely. Gently crack eggshells; peel under cold running water. Cut each egg in half lengthwise. Remove yolks. Press yolks through a sieve into a bowl. Set aside 1 tablespoon yolks. Combine 1 teaspoon lemon juice, remaining yolks, ¼ teaspoon salt, and pepper in a bowl; gradually add oil, stirring well with a whisk. Stir in yogurt. Add crabmeat, celery, and mustard; stir gently until combined. Taste filling; adjust seasoning, if necessary.
3. Arrange 3 lettuce leaves on each of 8 plates. Cut a thin slice from bottom of each egg white half. Pile crab filling evenly into egg white halves. Place 2 egg white halves on each plate. Sprinkle reserved yolk over egg white halves. Arrange ¼ cup radish mixture on the other side of each serving. Yield: 8 servings.

CALORIES 140; **FAT** 9.1g (sat 2.1g, mono 4.4g, poly 1.1g); **PROTEIN** 11.5g; **CARB** 4g; **FIBER** 1.3g; **CHOL** 237mg; **IRON** 2mg; **SODIUM** 411mg; **CALC** 72mg

Make salad for lunch or dinner with something from the sea: Fish and shellfish cook quickly (and if you use canned seafood, there's no cooking). As a lean source of protein, they provide all sorts of health benefits, including heart-healthy omega-3 fatty acids. Here's a guide to finding and preparing some of the seafood in this chapter.

PACIFIC SALMON

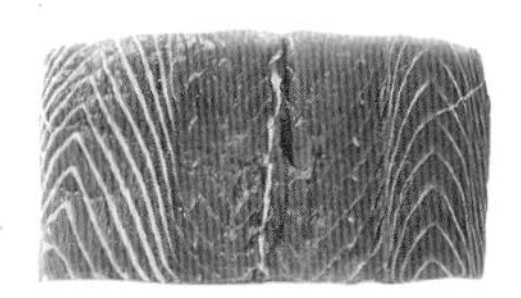

Choose wild Pacific salmon, especially Alaskan salmon, if you are concerned about sustainability. Alaskan salmon populations and fisheries are very well managed. Salmon's high fat content keeps it moist even when slightly overcooked—so it's a perfect option for the intense heat of the grill.

CRAB

Most salads in this collection call for lump crabmeat. When buying crabmeat, the meat should have a white or creamy color; skip meat that looks gray or blue. Smell the meat, as you would any seafood. Quality crabmeat should smell like the ocean, and the texture should feel firm and moist. Be sure to remove pieces of shell before using crabmeat in recipes.

SHRIMP

Finding sustainable shrimp is tricky: Wild shrimp are often caught with damaging trawling gear, and farmed shrimp can be tainted. One standard for sustainable shrimp is set by the Marine Stewardship Council—look for the Council's blue-and-white check mark on packaging. As a default choice, stick with U.S. or Canadian shrimp.

SCALLOPS

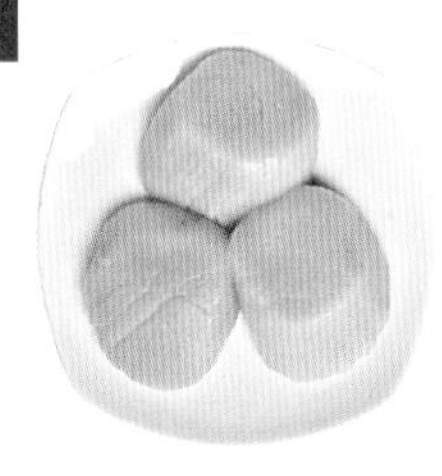

Poor-quality scallops are often treated with a saline solution; they'll look uniformly white and wet. Instead, look for a fishmonger offering "dry-packed" scallops. These haven't been treated and will vary in color from creamy to light orange. Before cooking, be sure to remove the small muscle from the side of the scallop if it's still attached, and pat the scallops dry.

MUSSELS

Mussels are relatively inexpensive, and they're also environmentally friendly. Because farmed mussels are grown suspended in water, there is no dredging the ocean floor to harvest them. To make sure mussels are alive, tap them to see if their shells close. Toss any mussels that do not close. Mussels cook quickly and can be steamed, smoked, grilled, and baked.

LOBSTER

Succulent lobster is available year-round and is least expensive during summer and early autumn. A live lobster should curl its tail under its body when picked up. Cook the lobster as soon as possible after purchasing. You may store it in the refrigerator for a few hours in a cardboard box or paper bag covered with wet newspaper. The lobster should still be alive when you begin to cook it; some cooks kill the lobster immediately before cooking.

CARIBBEAN SHRIMP SALAD WITH LIME VINAIGRETTE

4 cups chopped cooked shrimp
4 tablespoons seasoned rice vinegar, divided
1 tablespoon chili garlic sauce
1½ tablespoons olive oil
1 tablespoon grated lime rind
¼ cup fresh lime juice
½ teaspoon paprika
½ teaspoon ground cumin
2 garlic cloves, minced
Dash of salt
8 cups fresh baby spinach
1 cup sliced peeled mango
1 cup julienne-cut radishes
¼ cup diced peeled avocado
½ cup thinly sliced green onions
2 tablespoons unsalted pumpkinseed kernels, toasted

1. Combine shrimp, 1 tablespoon vinegar, and chili garlic sauce; toss well. Cover and chill 1 hour.
2. Combine 3 tablespoons vinegar, oil, and next 6 ingredients (through salt), stirring with a whisk.
3. Arrange 2 cups spinach on each of 4 plates; top each serving with 1 cup shrimp mixture. Arrange ¼ cup mango, ¼ cup radishes, 1 tablespoon avocado, 2 tablespoons green onions, and 1½ teaspoons pumpkinseed kernels on each plate. Drizzle each salad with 2 tablespoons vinaigrette. Yield: 4 servings.

CALORIES 215; **FAT** 7g (sat 1.1g, mono 3.8g, poly 1.7g); **PROTEIN** 26.2g; **CARB** 12.2g; **FIBER** 2.9g; **CHOL** 221mg; **IRON** 5.2mg; **SODIUM** 602mg; **CALC** 93mg

MANGOES

This tropical treat comes in season from May through September; look for large, smooth yellow fruit with a red blush.

MAKE-AHEAD

CRAB AND GRILLED CORN SALAD

Corn and crab are a popular combo for a good reason: They complement each other's sweetness so well. Here, grilling the corn intensifies that sweet flavor, and a creamy dressing with the zing of lime brings it all together. You can make the crab and corn salad ahead; wait until you're ready to serve before topping the lettuce with the crab mixture.

6 ears shucked corn
1 cup finely chopped celery
1 cup chopped bottled roasted red bell peppers, rinsed and drained
1/2 cup chopped fresh cilantro
1/3 cup thinly sliced green onions
12 ounces lump crabmeat, shell pieces removed
1/4 cup fresh lime juice
3 tablespoons canola mayonnaise
1/2 teaspoon freshly ground black pepper
3/8 teaspoon salt
1/8 teaspoon ground red pepper
12 Boston lettuce leaves

1. Heat a large grill pan over medium-high heat. Place corn in pan; cook 8 minutes or until slightly charred, turning frequently. Cool slightly. Cut kernels from ears of corn; place in a large bowl. Add celery and next 4 ingredients (through crabmeat) to corn; toss gently to combine.
2. Combine lime juice and next 4 ingredients (through red pepper) in a small bowl, stirring well with a whisk. Pour dressing over crab mixture; toss gently to coat. Serve salad over lettuce leaves. Yield: 6 servings (serving size: 1⅓ cups salad and 2 lettuce leaves).

CALORIES 249; **FAT** 8.3g (sat 0.6g, mono 2.4g, poly 4.7g); **PROTEIN** 16.8g; **CARB** 31g; **FIBER** 4.9g; **CHOL** 59mg; **IRON** 1.9mg; **SODIUM** 475mg; **CALC** 90mg

SHRIMP, AVOCADO, AND GRAPEFRUIT SALAD

2 1/2 tablespoons olive oil, divided
12 ounces peeled and deveined medium shrimp
1/2 teaspoon salt, divided
1/4 teaspoon freshly ground black pepper, divided
1 grapefruit
2 tablespoons chopped fresh tarragon
2 teaspoons brown sugar
1 teaspoon chopped shallots
6 cups chopped romaine lettuce
1 peeled avocado, cut into 12 wedges

1. Heat a large skillet over medium-high heat. Add 1½ teaspoons oil to pan; swirl to coat. Sprinkle shrimp with ¼ teaspoon salt and ⅛ teaspoon pepper. Add shrimp to pan; cook 3 minutes or until shrimp are done, stirring frequently. Remove from pan; keep warm.
2. Peel and section grapefruit over a bowl, reserving 3 tablespoons juice. Combine grapefruit juice, 2 tablespoons oil, ¼ teaspoon salt, ⅛ teaspoon pepper, tarragon, brown sugar, and shallots in a large bowl, stirring well with a whisk. Add lettuce; toss. Arrange 1½ cups lettuce mixture on each of 4 plates. Top each serving with 3 avocado wedges; divide shrimp and grapefruit sections evenly among servings. Yield: 4 servings.

CALORIES 291; **FAT** 17.7g (sat 2.6g, mono 11.3g, poly 2.5g); **PROTEIN** 19.9g; **CARB** 15.5g; **FIBER** 6g; **CHOL** 129mg; **IRON** 3.4mg; **SODIUM** 433mg; **CALC** 96mg

CRISPY CHICKPEA SALAD WITH GRILLED PRAWNS

Too cold to grill? Broil the skewers, or cook them on the stovetop in a grill pan. Substitute shrimp if you can't find prawns.

¼ cup extra-virgin olive oil, divided
4 teaspoons grated lemon rind, divided
¼ cup fresh lemon juice, divided
1 tablespoon chopped fresh flat-leaf parsley
2½ teaspoons crushed red pepper, divided
½ teaspoon salt, divided
½ teaspoon freshly ground black pepper
1 garlic clove, minced
36 large prawns, peeled and deveined (about 1½ pounds)
6 cups canola oil
3 cups rinsed and drained canned chickpeas (garbanzo beans)
Cooking spray
4 cups fresh baby arugula
2 cups fresh baby spinach
½ cup torn mint leaves
⅓ cup fresh flat-leaf parsley leaves
⅓ cup (¼-inch) diagonally cut green onions

1. Combine 1 tablespoon olive oil, 1½ teaspoons lemon rind, 1 tablespoon juice, parsley, 1 teaspoon red pepper, ¼ teaspoon salt, black pepper, and garlic in a medium bowl. Add shrimp; toss well. Marinate in refrigerator 1 hour, stirring occasionally.

2. Clip a candy/fry thermometer onto the side of a Dutch oven. Add canola oil to pan; heat oil to 385°.

3. Dry chickpeas thoroughly in a single layer on paper towels. Place 1½ cups chickpeas in hot oil; fry 4 minutes or until crisp, stirring occasionally. Make sure oil temperature remains at 375°. Remove peas from pan using a slotted spoon; drain on paper towels. Keep warm. Return oil to 385°. Repeat procedure with remaining chickpeas.

4. Remove shrimp from marinade; discard marinade. Thread 3 shrimp onto each of 12 (5-inch) skewers.

5. Preheat grill to medium-high heat.

6. Place skewers on grill rack coated with cooking spray. Grill shrimp 2½ minutes on each side or until done.

7. Combine 3 tablespoons olive oil, 2½ teaspoons lemon rind, 3 tablespoons juice, 1½ teaspoons red pepper, and ¼ teaspoon salt in a large bowl; stir with a whisk. Add chickpeas, arugula, spinach, and next 3 ingredients (through green onions); toss gently to combine. Place 1¼ cups chickpea mixture in each of 6 shallow bowls. Top each serving with 6 grilled shrimp. Yield: 6 servings.

CALORIES 272; **FAT** 16.5g (sat 1.8g, mono 9.7g, poly 2.8g); **PROTEIN** 11.7g; **CARB** 21.5g; **FIBER** 5.6g; **CHOL** 53mg; **IRON** 2.2mg; **SODIUM** 597mg; **CALC** 91mg

SUPERFAST

GRILLED SALMON AND SPINACH SALAD

Make the sweet citrus vinaigrette earlier in the day and store it in the refrigerator.

Vinaigrette:

1/4 cup fresh orange juice
2 tablespoons olive oil
2 tablespoons balsamic blend seasoned rice vinegar
1/2 teaspoon honey mustard
1/2 teaspoon freshly ground black pepper
1 garlic clove, minced

Salad:

2 tablespoons fresh lemon juice
4 (6-ounce) salmon fillets (about 1 inch thick)
2 teaspoons freshly ground black pepper
Cooking spray
1 (6-ounce) package fresh spinach
4 oranges, sectioned

1. Preheat grill to medium-high heat.
2. To prepare vinaigrette, combine first 6 ingredients in a large bowl; stir well with a whisk.
3. To prepare salad, drizzle lemon juice over fish; sprinkle with 2 teaspoons pepper. Place fish, skin sides up, on grill rack coated with cooking spray; grill 5 minutes on each side or until fish flakes easily when tested with a fork or until desired degree of doneness. Remove skin from fish; discard.
4. Add spinach to vinaigrette in bowl; toss well. Place 2 cups spinach mixture on each of 4 plates; arrange 1 piece fish on each plate. Divide orange sections evenly among 4 plates. Yield: 4 servings.

CALORIES 474; **FAT** 25.7g (sat 4.7g, mono 11.6g, poly 7.7g); **PROTEIN** 36.2g; **CARB** 27.5g; **FIBER** 8.4g; **CHOL** 100mg; **IRON** 2.5mg; **SODIUM** 286mg; **CALC** 129mg

SUPERFAST

GRILLED SCALLOP SALAD

Grill scallops and cucumber for tasty toppings on this summer salad. All scallops, whether farmed, diver-caught, or wild-caught, are great sustainable seafood options.

1/2 teaspoon freshly ground black pepper, divided
3/8 teaspoon salt, divided
12 large sea scallops (about 1 1/2 pounds)
1 English cucumber, halved lengthwise
Cooking spray
2 tablespoons fresh lime juice
2 teaspoons extra-virgin olive oil
4 cups torn romaine lettuce
3 cups (1-inch) cubed seedless watermelon
1/4 cup torn mint leaves
1/2 peeled avocado, cut into 8 slices

1. Preheat grill to medium-high heat.
2. Sprinkle ¼ teaspoon pepper and ¼ teaspoon salt over scallops and cucumber. Arrange in a single layer on grill rack coated with cooking spray. Grill 3 minutes on each side or until scallops are done and cucumber is well marked. Remove from heat; cut cucumber into ¼-inch slices.
3. Combine ⅛ teaspoon salt, juice, and oil in a large bowl; stir with a whisk. Add cucumber, lettuce, watermelon, and mint; toss gently to coat. Divide watermelon mixture evenly among 4 plates. Top each serving with 3 scallops and 2 avocado slices. Sprinkle evenly with ¼ teaspoon freshly ground black pepper. Yield: 4 servings.

CALORIES 263; **FAT** 7.5g (sat 1g, mono 4.2g, poly 1.3g); **PROTEIN** 31.4g; **CARB** 18.6g; **FIBER** 3.7g; **CHOL** 56mg; **IRON** 2mg; **SODIUM** 501mg; **CALC** 92mg

HERBED SHRIMP AND WHITE BEAN SALAD

Shrimp star in this main-course salad full of colorful veggies and topped with a lemon juice vinaigrette.

1 red bell pepper
4 cups arugula, loosely packed
½ cup thinly vertically sliced red onion
2 tablespoons chopped fresh chives
2 tablespoons chopped fresh basil
1 tablespoon chopped fresh flat-leaf parsley
1 (15-ounce) can cannellini beans or other white beans, rinsed and drained
½ teaspoon grated lemon rind
2 tablespoons fresh lemon juice
1 garlic clove, minced
3 tablespoons extra-virgin olive oil
¼ teaspoon salt, divided
¼ teaspoon freshly ground black pepper, divided
Cooking spray
1 pound peeled and deveined large shrimp
2 tablespoons pine nuts, toasted

1. Preheat broiler.

2. Cut bell pepper in half lengthwise; discard seeds and membranes. Place halves, skin sides up, on a baking sheet. Broil 12 minutes or until blackened. Place in a paper bag, and seal. Let stand 5 minutes. Peel; chop. Combine bell pepper, arugula, and next 5 ingredients (through beans). Combine rind, juice, garlic, oil, ⅛ teaspoon salt, and ⅛ teaspoon pepper.

3. Heat a large skillet over medium-high heat. Coat pan with cooking spray. Sprinkle shrimp with remaining salt and pepper. Cook 2 minutes on each side or until done. Add shrimp, lemon mixture, and nuts to arugula mixture; toss. Yield: 4 servings (serving size: 2 cups).

CALORIES 326; **FAT** 15.7g (sat 2.1g, mono 9.2g, poly 3.3g); **PROTEIN** 28.9g; **CARB** 17.4g; **FIBER** 4.8g; **CHOL** 172mg; **IRON** 4.5mg; **SODIUM** 494mg; **CALC** 136mg

LIME SHRIMP SALAD WITH BEAN SPROUTS AND THAI BASIL

This refreshing salad gets its flavor from an oil-free, boldly seasoned dressing.

Salad:

2 cups fresh bean sprouts
2 cups thinly sliced napa (Chinese) cabbage
1 cup diced fresh pineapple
3/4 cup shredded carrot (about 1 large)
1/2 cup coarsely chopped fresh mint leaves
1/4 cup coarsely chopped Thai basil leaves
5 cups water
3/4 pound medium shrimp, peeled and deveined

Dressing:

1 tablespoon brown sugar
3 tablespoons fresh lime juice (about 1 lime)
2 tablespoons fish sauce
2 garlic cloves, minced
2 Thai chiles, seeded and minced
3/4 cup chopped unsalted, dry-roasted peanuts
Lime wedges (optional)

1. To prepare salad, combine first 6 ingredients in a large bowl.

2. Bring 5 cups water to a boil in a large saucepan. Add shrimp to pan; reduce heat, and simmer 2 minutes or until done. Drain and rinse shrimp under cold water; drain well. Cut shrimp in half lengthwise; add shrimp to sprouts mixture, tossing to combine.

3. To prepare dressing, combine sugar and next 4 ingredients (through chiles) in a small bowl, stirring with a whisk until sugar dissolves. Pour dressing over salad, tossing to coat. Sprinkle with peanuts. Serve with lime wedges, if desired. Yield: 6 servings (serving size: 1 cup shrimp salad and 2 tablespoons peanuts).

CALORIES 221; **FAT** 10.3g (sat 1.5g, mono 4.7g, poly 3.3g); **PROTEIN** 18.3g; **CARB** 16.5g; **FIBER** 3.3g; **CHOL** 86mg; **IRON** 2.6mg; **SODIUM** 565mg; **CALC** 82mg

THAI BASIL

Thai basil has a purple hue on its stems and a licorice flavor.

MAKE-AHEAD / PORTABLE / SUPERFAST

LEMON-SPLASHED SHRIMP SALAD

You can purchase peeled and deveined shrimp to save prep time. Chop, measure, and prepare the remaining ingredients while the pasta water comes to a boil.

8 cups water
2/3 cup uncooked rotini (corkscrew pasta)
1 1/2 pounds peeled and deveined large shrimp
1 cup halved cherry tomatoes
3/4 cup sliced celery
1/2 cup chopped avocado
1/2 cup chopped seeded poblano pepper
2 tablespoons chopped fresh cilantro
2 teaspoons grated lemon rind
3 tablespoons fresh lemon juice
2 teaspoons extra-virgin olive oil
1/2 teaspoon kosher salt

1. Bring 8 cups water to a boil in a large saucepan. Add pasta to pan; cook 5 minutes or until al dente. Add shrimp; cook 3 minutes or until done. Drain. Rinse with cold water; drain well.

2. Combine pasta mixture, tomatoes, and remaining ingredients; toss well. Yield: 4 servings (serving size: about 1¾ cups).

CALORIES 250; **FAT** 6.9g (sat 1.2g, mono 3.8g, poly 1.2g); **PROTEIN** 30.3g; **CARB** 17g; **FIBER** 2.6g; **CHOL** 252mg; **IRON** 5.1mg; **SODIUM** 547mg; **CALC** 74mg

MIXED SEAFOOD SALAD

If you can extract lobster meat from the claw whole, it will make a pretty presentation; otherwise, chop it with the rest of the lobster meat.

1½ cups water
6 tablespoons fresh lemon juice (about 2 lemons), divided
1½ pounds mussels, scrubbed and debearded
½ pound peeled and deveined shrimp
½ pound cleaned skinless squid
1 (1¼-pound) wild American lobster
⅛ teaspoon kosher salt
¼ teaspoon freshly ground black pepper
2 tablespoons extra-virgin olive oil
2 cups fresh cilantro leaves
1 cup thinly sliced radicchio
1½ cups thinly sliced celery
1 cup thinly sliced red onion
¼ teaspoon crushed red pepper
1 head frisée, torn

1. Bring 1½ cups water and 3 tablespoons juice to a boil in a Dutch oven. Add mussels; cover and cook 2 minutes or until shells open. Remove mussels from pan with a slotted spoon; discard any unopened shells. Cool. Remove meat from mussels; discard shells. Place meat in a large bowl.

2. Add shrimp to boiling liquid in pan; cook 2 minutes or until done. Remove shrimp from pan with a slotted spoon, and add to mussel meat. Cut squid crosswise into ¼-inch rings, and leave tentacles whole. Add squid to boiling liquid in pan; cook 1 minute. Remove squid from pan with a slotted spoon. Cool; add squid to mussels mixture. Add lobster to pan; cover, reduce heat, and simmer 8 minutes. Remove lobster from pan, reserving 1 tablespoon cooking liquid; cool lobster. Remove meat from lobster tail and claws; coarsely chop. Add lobster, salt, and black pepper to mussels mixture.

3. Combine 3 tablespoons juice, reserved cooking liquid, and olive oil in a bowl, stirring with a whisk. Drizzle lemon mixture over seafood mixture; toss gently to coat. Cover and marinate in refrigerator 1½ hours. Combine seafood mixture, cilantro, and remaining ingredients, and toss gently. Yield: 4 servings (serving size: about 2 cups).

CALORIES 339; **FAT** 11.2g (sat 1.8g, mono 5.6g, poly 2.1g); **PROTEIN** 44.4g; **CARB** 14.5g; **FIBER** 4.7g; **CHOL** 283mg; **IRON** 6.7mg; **SODIUM** 683mg; **CALC** 192mg

SQUID

Buy calamari, or squid, fresh or frozen. If you're buying fresh, look for small squid, which are generally more tender. They should have clear eyes and a fresh ocean smell. Use them within a day. The key to preparing squid is to cook them until just done; any longer can cause them to turn rubbery.

SUPERFAST

SEARED SCALLOPS WITH FENNEL AND GRAPEFRUIT SALAD

Notes of citrus and licorice highlight the sweetness of the scallops.

2 large red grapefruit
3 cups thinly sliced fennel bulb (about 1 medium)
3/4 cup flat-leaf parsley leaves
1 tablespoon extra-virgin olive oil, divided
1/2 teaspoon kosher salt, divided
1 1/2 pounds large sea scallops
1/4 teaspoon freshly ground black pepper

1. Peel and section grapefruit over a bowl to measure 1½ cups sections; squeeze membranes to extract ½ cup juice. Set juice aside. Combine grapefruit sections, fennel, and parsley in a medium bowl. Add 2 teaspoons oil and ¼ teaspoon kosher salt; toss gently to combine.
2. Heat 1 teaspoon oil in a large nonstick skillet over medium-high heat. Sprinkle scallops with ¼ teaspoon kosher salt and ¼ teaspoon freshly ground black pepper. Add scallops to pan; cook 2 minutes on each side or until desired degree of doneness. Remove scallops from pan; keep warm.
3. Add reserved ½ cup juice to pan; cook until reduced to ¼ cup (about 2 minutes). Remove from heat. Place 1 cup fennel mixture on each of 4 plates. Divide scallops evenly among plates; top each serving with 1 tablespoon juice. Yield: 4 servings.

CALORIES 292; **FAT** 5g (sat 0.6g, mono 2.6g, poly 0.8g); **PROTEIN** 27g; **CARB** 37.4g; **FIBER** 5.7g; **CHOL** 47mg; **IRON** 2mg; **SODIUM** 507mg; **CALC** 122mg

FENNEL

Look for small, heavy, white fennel bulbs that are firm and free of cracks, browning, or moist areas. The stalks should be crisp, with bright-green fronds. Wrapped in plastic, fennel keeps for a few days in the refrigerator.

HOW TO

BUY THE BEST SEAFOOD

IT'S SO EASY TO FEEL overwhelmed at the fish counter. Which is tastiest? Which is healthiest? Which is the most sustainable choice? Partly because of all the confusion, more than half of Americans seldom, if ever, eat fish, and if they do, it's usually at a restaurant. That's unfortunate because fish and shellfish offer substantial health benefits. Moreover, they're easy to cook at home.

The basics

1 **Choose a quality seafood market:** Choose a seafood market with knowledgeable salespeople. Fish should be displayed attractively and surrounded by plenty of clean crushed ice.

2 **Be flexible:** The best approach to buying and eating seafood is to let freshness be your guide. It's easy to substitute one fish for another, so, for example, if the mahimahi looks and smells fresher than the pompano, buy it instead.

3 **Handle properly:** When shopping, ask the salesperson to pack your fish with a separate bag of crushed ice to keep it cold. Refrigerate whole fish up to two days, and fillets and steaks one to two days. Place the fish in a plastic bag, and then top with a zip-top plastic bag filled with ice. Thaw frozen fish in the refrigerator.

Whole fresh fish

- Look for shiny skin; tightly adhering scales; bright, clear eyes; firm, taut flesh that springs back when pressed; and a moist, flat tail.
- Gills should be cherry-red, not brownish.
- Saltwater fish should smell briny; freshwater fish should smell like a clean pond.

Fresh fillets and steaks

- When buying white-fleshed fish, choose translucent-looking fillets with a pinkish tint.
- When buying any color fish, the flesh should appear dense without any gaps between layers.
- If the fish is wrapped in plastic, the package should contain little to no liquid.

SESAME SHRIMP SALAD

More adventurous greens, such as napa cabbage and watercress, add texture. Shrimp are a source of omega-3s and protein that is low in saturated fat.

1 tablespoon sugar
3 tablespoons fresh lime juice, divided
1 tablespoon water
1 garlic clove, minced
2 teaspoons chili garlic sauce, divided
1 teaspoon fish sauce
¼ teaspoon salt, divided
1 tablespoon orange marmalade
2 teaspoons dark sesame oil, divided
24 large shrimp, peeled and deveined (about 1 pound)
5 cups shredded napa (Chinese) cabbage
1½ cups trimmed watercress leaves
1½ cups shredded carrot
⅓ cup chopped fresh cilantro
⅓ cup chopped fresh mint
2 tablespoons toasted sesame seeds

1. Combine sugar, 2 tablespoons juice, 1 tablespoon water, and garlic in a small microwave-safe bowl; cover with plastic wrap. Microwave at HIGH 40 seconds or until sugar dissolves. Cool. Stir in 1 teaspoon chili garlic sauce, fish sauce, and ⅛ teaspoon salt.

2. Combine 1 tablespoon juice, 1 teaspoon chili garlic sauce, marmalade, and 1 teaspoon oil in a large bowl, stirring with a whisk. Add shrimp to bowl; toss to coat. Marinate shrimp in refrigerator 15 minutes, tossing occasionally. Remove shrimp from bowl, reserving marinade. Thread 3 shrimp onto each of 8 (8-inch) wooden skewers.

3. Heat 1 teaspoon oil in a large nonstick skillet over medium-high heat. Add shrimp skewers and reserved marinade to pan; cook 3½ minutes or until shrimp are done and glazed, turning once.

4. Combine cabbage and next 5 ingredients (through sesame seeds) in a large bowl. Drizzle fish sauce mixture over cabbage mixture; toss well to coat. Arrange 2 cups cabbage mixture on each of 4 plates; top each serving with 2 skewers. Yield: 4 servings.

CALORIES 237; **FAT** 7.2g (sat 1.1g, mono 2.3g, poly 3g); **PROTEIN** 26.2g; **CARB** 17.7g; **FIBER** 3.3g; **CHOL** 172mg; **IRON** 3.3mg; **SODIUM** 518mg; **CALC** 176mg

SHRIMP COBB SALAD

Typical Cobb salads include chicken and hard-cooked eggs; this riff uses shrimp and corn.

4 center-cut bacon slices
1 pound large shrimp, peeled and deveined
½ teaspoon paprika
¼ teaspoon freshly ground black pepper
Cooking spray
¼ teaspoon salt, divided
2½ tablespoons fresh lemon juice
1½ tablespoons extra-virgin olive oil
½ teaspoon whole-grain Dijon mustard
1 (10-ounce) package romaine salad
2 cups cherry tomatoes, quartered
1 cup shredded carrot (about 2 large carrots)
1 cup frozen whole-kernel corn, thawed
1 ripe peeled avocado, cut into 8 wedges

1. Cook bacon in a large nonstick skillet over medium heat until crisp. Remove bacon from pan; cut in half crosswise. Wipe pan clean with paper towels. Increase heat to medium-high. Sprinkle shrimp with paprika and pepper. Coat pan with cooking spray. Add shrimp to pan; cook 2 minutes on each side or until done. Sprinkle with ⅛ teaspoon salt; toss to coat.
2. While shrimp cooks, combine ⅛ teaspoon salt, juice, oil, and mustard in a large bowl, stirring with a whisk. Add lettuce; toss to coat.
3. Arrange about 1½ cups lettuce mixture on each of 4 plates. Top each serving with about 6 shrimp, ½ cup tomatoes, ¼ cup carrot, ¼ cup corn, 2 avocado wedges, and 2 bacon pieces. Yield: 4 servings.

CALORIES 332; **FAT** 15.2g (sat 2.9g, mono 8g, poly 2.6g); **PROTEIN** 30g; **CARB** 21.8g; **FIBER** 7.5g; **CHOL** 181mg; **IRON** 4.3mg; **SODIUM** 551mg; **CALC** 110mg

AVOCADOS

Ripe avocados will give slightly when gently pressed at the stem end. You can ripen firm avocados in a paper bag at room temperature.

SHRIMP SALAD WITH BLOOD ORANGES AND SLIVERED FENNEL

U.S.-farmed or wild shrimp are good sustainable seafood choices. For pretty slivers of fennel, use a mandoline to slice the bulb.

1/4 cup fresh blood orange juice (about 1 orange)
1 tablespoon fresh lemon juice
2 tablespoons extra-virgin olive oil, divided
1/2 teaspoon sea salt, divided
1/4 teaspoon freshly ground black pepper
24 jumbo shrimp, peeled and deveined (about 1 1/2 pounds)
Cooking spray
3 blood oranges, peeled and cut crosswise into thin slices
2 cups thinly sliced fennel bulb (about 1 small)
Chopped fennel fronds (optional)

1. Combine orange juice, lemon juice, 1½ tablespoons oil, ¼ teaspoon salt, and pepper, stirring well with a whisk.
2. Preheat grill to medium-high heat.
3. Combine shrimp, 1½ teaspoons oil, and ¼ teaspoon salt; toss to coat. Thread 4 shrimp onto each of 6 (12-inch) skewers. Place skewers on grill rack coated with cooking spray; grill 3 minutes on each side or until done. Remove shrimp from skewers; keep warm.
4. Divide orange slices evenly among 4 plates; top each serving with ½ cup fennel and 6 shrimp. Drizzle 1 tablespoon dressing over each serving. Sprinkle with fennel fronds, if desired. Serve immediately. Yield: 4 servings.

CALORIES 329; **FAT** 9.8g (sat 1.5g, mono 5.4g, poly 1.9g); **PROTEIN** 36.3g; **CARB** 22.2g; **FIBER** 4.9g; **CHOL** 259mg; **IRON** 4.6mg; **SODIUM** 570mg; **CALC** 178mg

MAKE-AHEAD / SUPERFAST

SPICY CHIPOTLE SHRIMP SALAD ➤

Shrimp salad is an easy make-ahead meal. To keep the lettuce from wilting, wait until you're ready to serve before topping it with the shrimp salad. For a kid-friendly twist, substitute diced red bell pepper for the chiles.

1 1/2 pounds peeled and deveined large shrimp
1/8 teaspoon salt
1/8 teaspoon freshly ground black pepper
Cooking spray
1/4 cup finely chopped celery
2 tablespoons finely chopped red onion
2 tablespoons chopped fresh cilantro
3 tablespoons canola mayonnaise
1 tablespoon chopped chipotle chile, canned in adobo sauce
2 teaspoons fresh lime juice
1/2 teaspoon ground cumin
8 Boston lettuce leaves

1. Heat a grill pan over medium-high heat. Sprinkle shrimp with salt and black pepper. Coat pan with cooking spray. Add half of shrimp to pan; cook 2 minutes on each side or until done. Remove shrimp from pan; repeat procedure with remaining shrimp. Cool shrimp 5 minutes.
2. Place shrimp in a medium bowl; stir in celery and next 6 ingredients (through cumin). Arrange 2 lettuce leaves on each of 4 plates; top each serving with ¾ cup shrimp mixture. Yield: 4 servings.

CALORIES 235; **FAT** 10.9g (sat 0.9g, mono 3g, poly 6.2g); **PROTEIN** 29.2g; **CARB** 3.2g; **FIBER** 0.8g; **CHOL** 219mg; **IRON** 3.8mg; **SODIUM** 400mg; **CALC** 87mg

MAKE-AHEAD / SUPERFAST

SPICY CRAB-PAPAYA SALAD

This salad is a tropical combination with sweet and spicy notes.

1½ cups diced seeded peeled papaya
⅓ cup thinly sliced green onions
¼ cup thinly sliced celery
1 thinly sliced jalapeño pepper
1 pound lump crabmeat (shell pieces removed)
3 tablespoons canola oil
2 tablespoons cider vinegar
2 teaspoons sugar
1 teaspoon Dijon mustard
¼ teaspoon freshly ground black pepper
⅛ teaspoon salt

1. Combine first 5 ingredients in a large bowl.
2. Combine canola oil and next 5 ingredients (through salt) in a small bowl, stirring with a whisk. Drizzle vinegar mixture over crab mixture; toss. Chill. Yield: 4 servings (serving size: 1 cup).

CALORIES 246; **FAT** 12.6g (sat 1.1g, mono 7g, poly 3.8g); **PROTEIN** 23.3g; **CARB** 8.7g; **FIBER** 1.5g; **CHOL** 113mg; **IRON** 1.3mg; **SODIUM** 430mg; **CALC** 141mg

PAPAYAS

When shopping for papayas, look for vibrantly colored fruit that gives a little to pressure. Ripen slightly green papayas in a paper bag at room temperature; store them in the refrigerator once ripe. The dark seeds inside the fruit are edible, too.

SUPERFAST

THAI SEAFOOD SALAD

Substitute one of the shellfish with whatever you have on hand or what looks good in the market.

1/4 cup water
8 ounces sea scallops
1 pound peeled and deveined medium shrimp
5 tablespoons fresh lime juice
1 1/2 tablespoons fish sauce
1 teaspoon sugar
1 teaspoon chile paste with garlic
1 cup red bell pepper strips
1/2 cup thinly vertically sliced red onion
1/4 cup torn mint leaves
8 ounces lump crabmeat, drained and shell pieces removed
2 fresh lemongrass stalks, trimmed and thinly sliced
1 cucumber, halved lengthwise and thinly sliced

1. Bring ¼ cup water to a simmer in a large skillet. Add scallops to pan; cover and cook 3 minutes or until done. Remove scallops from pan with a slotted spoon; pat scallops dry with paper towels. Place scallops in a large bowl. Add shrimp to simmering water in pan; cover and cook 3 minutes or until done. Drain well; add to scallops.

2. While scallops and shrimp cook, combine lime juice, fish sauce, sugar, and chile paste; stir to dissolve sugar.

3. Combine scallop mixture, juice mixture, bell pepper, and remaining ingredients; toss gently. Yield: 6 servings (serving size: about 1⅓ cups).

CALORIES 182; **FAT** 2.3g (sat 0.4g, mono 0.3g, poly 0.9g); **PROTEIN** 30.7g; **CARB** 8.9g; **FIBER** 0.9g; **CHOL** 165mg; **IRON** 3mg; **SODIUM** 566mg; **CALC** 108mg

LEMONGRASS

This herb is long and thin, with a citrus-like flavor. Look for it in the produce section of your supermarket or in Asian markets. Remove the outer leaves and dark-green leafy tops to reveal the creamy bulb, which you can chop, crush, slice, or grate. The tender green stalk is nice thinly sliced for salads.

TIGER PRAWN, NOODLE, AND HERB SALAD

A beautiful and delicious starter, this Asian-influenced noodle dish offers a different interpretation of shrimp on the barbie. Here, some Vietnamese influences pair with Australia's moist, sweet tiger prawns. Substitute shrimp if you can't find prawns. Use a different variety of mint, such as Vietnamese mint.

1/4 cup fresh lime juice
1 tablespoon palm sugar or brown sugar
1 tablespoon fish sauce
2 garlic cloves, crushed
12 tiger prawns (about 20 ounces)
Cooking spray
2 ounces rice vermicelli
1/2 cup thinly diagonally sliced green onions
1/2 cup loosely packed cilantro leaves
1/2 cup loosely packed torn mint leaves
1/4 cup shredded unsweetened coconut
1/4 cup chopped salted, dry-roasted peanuts
2 Thai chiles, thinly sliced

1. Combine first 4 ingredients in a medium bowl, stirring until sugar dissolves. Let stand 30 minutes; discard garlic.
2. Preheat grill to medium-high heat.
3. Peel prawns, leaving tails intact. Arrange prawns on grill rack coated with cooking spray; grill 4 minutes or until done, turning once.
4. Cook noodles according to package directions. Combine noodles, green onions, and next 5 ingredients (through chiles) in a large bowl. Drizzle with juice mixture, tossing to coat. Top with prawns. Yield: 6 servings (serving size: ½ cup noodle mixture and 2 prawns).

CALORIES 128; **FAT** 5.1g (sat 2.5g, mono 1.2g, poly 0.9g); **PROTEIN** 5.4g; **CARB** 15.8g; **FIBER** 1.8g; **CHOL** 21mg; **IRON** 1.2mg; **SODIUM** 260mg; **CALC** 33mg

PORTABLE

TOMATO PANZANELLA WITH SHRIMP AND BASIL

Use multicolored heirloom tomatoes when they're in season for a pretty plate.

4 cups (3/4-inch) cubed whole-wheat French bread baguette (about 6 ounces)
5 cups ripe tomato wedges (about 4 large)
1/2 teaspoon kosher salt, divided
1/2 pound medium shrimp, peeled and deveined
1/4 teaspoon freshly ground black pepper
2 tablespoons olive oil
1/4 teaspoon crushed red pepper
6 garlic cloves, thinly sliced
1 tablespoon fresh lemon juice
1 1/2 cups small fresh basil leaves

1. Preheat oven to 375°.
2. Place bread cubes on a jelly-roll pan. Bake at 375° for 20 minutes or until crisp and golden brown, turning cubes once.
3. Combine tomatoes and ¼ teaspoon salt in a large bowl. Sprinkle shrimp with ¼ teaspoon salt and black pepper. Heat olive oil, red pepper, and garlic in a large nonstick skillet over low heat; cook 5 minutes or until warm and fragrant. Increase heat to medium-high. Add shrimp to pan; sauté 2 minutes or until shrimp are done, stirring frequently. Stir in lemon juice. Add bread, shrimp mixture, and basil to tomatoes; toss gently to coat. Let stand 5 minutes before serving. Yield: 4 servings (serving size: 2½ cups).

CALORIES 272; **FAT** 8.7g (sat 1.2g, mono 5.2g, poly 1.4g); **PROTEIN** 17.9g; **CARB** 30.9g; **FIBER** 3.8g; **CHOL** 86mg; **IRON** 3.7mg; **SODIUM** 557mg; **CALC** 89mg

SOUTHWESTERN-STYLE SHRIMP TACO SALAD

Cilantro, chipotle hot sauce, corn, black beans, and green onions lend fantastic south-of-the-border flavor to this shrimp-topped taco salad.

1/4 cup fresh lime juice
2 tablespoons olive oil
1 teaspoon ground cumin
2 teaspoons minced garlic
2 teaspoons maple syrup
2 teaspoons chipotle hot sauce
3/4 pound medium shrimp, peeled and deveined
2 ears shucked corn
Cooking spray
1 cup chopped romaine lettuce
1/2 cup chopped green onions
1/4 cup chopped fresh cilantro
1 (15-ounce) can black beans, rinsed and drained
3 plum tomatoes, chopped
2 ounces baked blue corn tortilla chips (about 1 1/2 cups)
1/3 cup light sour cream
1/4 cup diced peeled avocado
Lime wedges (optional)

1. Preheat grill to medium-high heat.
2. Combine lime juice and next 5 ingredients (through hot sauce) in a small bowl, stirring with a whisk. Place shrimp in a shallow bowl. Drizzle 1 tablespoon lime juice mixture over shrimp, tossing gently to coat. Reserve remaining lime juice mixture; set aside. Thread shrimp onto metal skewers. Lightly coat corn with cooking spray. Place shrimp kebabs and corn on grill rack coated with cooking spray. Grill 8 minutes, turning kebabs once and turning corn frequently until browned. Remove from grill; cool slightly.
3. Remove shrimp from skewers, and place in a large bowl. Cut kernels from ears of corn. Add corn, chopped lettuce, green onions, cilantro, black beans, and plum tomatoes to shrimp. Drizzle reserved lime juice mixture over shrimp mixture, and toss gently to combine.
4. Divide tortilla chips evenly among 6 shallow bowls; top each serving with 1 cup shrimp mixture. Combine sour cream and diced avocado in a small bowl; mash with a fork until well blended. Top each serving with about 1 tablespoon sour cream mixture. Serve with a lime wedge, if desired. Yield: 6 servings.

CALORIES 228; **FAT** 8.5g (sat 1.8g, mono 4.4g, poly 1.4g); **PROTEIN** 16.2g; **CARB** 25.5g; **FIBER** 4.5g; **CHOL** 91mg; **IRON** 2.7mg; **SODIUM** 327mg; **CALC** 79mg

MAKE-AHEAD / PORTABLE

ARUGULA, ITALIAN TUNA, AND WHITE BEAN SALAD ➤

This no-cook dinner recipe is packed with colorful vegetables and gets a flavor kick from its zesty vinaigrette.

3 tablespoons fresh lemon juice
1 1/2 tablespoons extra-virgin olive oil
1/2 teaspoon minced garlic
1/8 teaspoon kosher salt
1/4 teaspoon freshly ground black pepper
1/4 teaspoon Dijon mustard
1 cup grape tomatoes, halved
1 cup thinly vertically sliced red onion
2 (6-ounce) cans Italian tuna packed in olive oil, drained and broken into chunks
1 (15-ounce) can cannellini beans, rinsed and drained
1 (5-ounce) package fresh baby arugula
2 ounces shaved fresh Parmigiano-Reggiano cheese

1. Combine first 6 ingredients in a large bowl, stirring with a whisk.
2. Add tomatoes and next 4 ingredients (through arugula); toss. Top with cheese. Yield: 4 servings (serving size: 2 1/4 cups).

CALORIES 301; **FAT** 14.5g (sat 4.1g, mono 6.7g, poly 2.8g); **PROTEIN** 27.5g; **CARB** 15g; **FIBER** 3.8g; **CHOL** 21mg; **IRON** 2.5mg; **SODIUM** 562mg; **CALC** 263mg

MEDITERRANEAN SALMON SALAD

In a pinch, use canned drained wild sockeye salmon—and flake with two forks—in place of the sautéed fillets.

½ cup uncooked orzo
2 (6-ounce) salmon fillets (about 1 inch thick)
¼ teaspoon salt
¼ teaspoon dried oregano
⅛ teaspoon freshly ground black pepper
Cooking spray
2 cups torn spinach
½ cup chopped red bell pepper
¼ cup chopped green onions
4 kalamata olives, pitted and chopped
3 tablespoons fresh lemon juice
2 tablespoons crumbled feta cheese

1. Preheat broiler.
2. Cook pasta according to package directions, omitting salt and fat.
3. Sprinkle fish evenly with salt, oregano, and black pepper. Place fish on a broiler pan coated with cooking spray. Broil 10 minutes or until fish flakes easily when tested with a fork or until desired degree of doneness. Let stand 5 minutes; break into bite-sized pieces with 2 forks.
4. Combine pasta, fish, spinach, and remaining ingredients in a medium bowl; toss well.
Yield: 4 servings (serving size: 1 cup).

CALORIES 231; **FAT** 7.7g (sat 1.6g, mono 2.7g, poly 2.3g); **PROTEIN** 20.3g; **CARB** 19.3g; **FIBER** 1.8g; **CHOL** 49mg; **IRON** 1.3mg; **SODIUM** 310mg; **CALC** 56mg

KALAMATA OLIVES

Some olives are best for making oil; others, table olives, are best for eating. The kalamata, a table olive from Greece, is cured in a brine. Jarred olives will keep for two weeks after you open them.

SUPERFAST

PAN-GRILLED THAI TUNA SALAD

Pair with a side of crunchy rice crackers. A citrusy dessert makes an excellent follow-up after the spicy salad.

Cooking spray
2 (6-ounce) yellowfin tuna steaks (about 1 inch thick)
1/4 teaspoon salt
1/8 teaspoon freshly ground black pepper
4 cups thinly sliced napa (Chinese) cabbage
1 cup thinly sliced cucumber
1/2 cup matchstick-cut carrots
1/3 cup presliced red onion
1 medium navel orange, sectioned and chopped
1 tablespoon sugar
2 tablespoons chopped fresh cilantro
2 tablespoons fresh lime juice
2 tablespoons rice vinegar
1/2 teaspoon dark sesame oil
1/4 teaspoon sambal oelek (ground fresh chile paste) or Sriracha (hot chile sauce)

1. Heat a grill pan over medium-high heat. Coat pan with cooking spray. Sprinkle fish evenly with salt and pepper. Add fish to pan; cook 2 minutes on each side or until desired degree of doneness. Transfer to a cutting board.

2. Combine cabbage and next 4 ingredients in a large bowl (through orange). Combine sugar and next 5 ingredients (through sambal oelek) in a small bowl, stirring well with a whisk. Reserve 1 tablespoon dressing. Drizzle remaining dressing over salad; toss gently to coat. Divide salad mixture evenly between 2 plates. Cut each tuna steak across grain into ¼-inch slices; arrange over salad mixture. Drizzle 1½ teaspoons reserved dressing over each serving. Yield: 2 servings.

CALORIES 307; **FAT** 3g (sat 0.6g, mono 0.8g, poly 1g); **PROTEIN** 41.8g; **CARB** 28.4g; **FIBER** 5.2g; **CHOL** 74mg; **IRON** 1.6mg; **SODIUM** 398mg; **CALC** 201mg

SUPERFAST

SAUTÉED ARCTIC CHAR AND ARUGULA SALAD WITH TOMATO VINAIGRETTE

If you can't find arctic char, substitute another environmentally friendly option, such as Alaskan salmon.

4 (6-ounce) arctic char fillets
3/4 teaspoon salt, divided
1/2 teaspoon freshly ground black pepper, divided
Cooking spray
4 teaspoons balsamic vinegar
2 tablespoons extra-virgin olive oil
2 teaspoons minced shallots
1 pint grape tomatoes, halved
5 cups loosely packed arugula
2 tablespoons pine nuts, toasted

1. Heat a large nonstick skillet over medium-high heat. Sprinkle fish evenly with ½ teaspoon salt and ¼ teaspoon pepper. Coat pan with cooking spray. Add fish to pan; cook 3 minutes or until browned. Turn fish over; cook 4 minutes or until desired degree of doneness. Remove fish from pan; loosely cover, and keep warm. Wipe pan clean with paper towels.
2. While fish cooks, place vinegar in a medium bowl. Gradually add oil, stirring with a whisk. Stir in shallots.
3. Return pan to medium-high heat. Add tomatoes, ¼ teaspoon salt, and ¼ teaspoon black pepper; sauté 3 minutes or until tomatoes soften. Add tomatoes to vinaigrette; toss to combine.
4. Arrange 1¼ cups arugula on each of 4 plates; top each serving with 1 fish fillet. Spoon about ½ cup tomato mixture over each salad, and sprinkle with 1½ teaspoons nuts. Yield: 4 servings.

CALORIES 342; **FAT** 20.5g (sat 3.7g, mono 10.4g, poly 4.8g); **PROTEIN** 33.1g; **CARB** 5.9g; **FIBER** 1.6g; **CHOL** 80mg; **IRON** 1.5mg; **SODIUM** 522mg; **CALC** 72mg

ARCTIC CHAR

Closely related to salmon, arctic char is high in omega-3s and has a mild flavor. Most char sold in the U.S. is sustainably farmed. It ranges in color from white to orange, depending upon what it is fed.

◀ SMOKED TROUT AND NEW POTATO SALAD

This twist on a favorite picnic side dish gains distinctive character from smoked trout and fresh herbs. Make it a few hours ahead, if you like. Serve with grilled pork or chicken.

1 pound small red potatoes, quartered
1/2 cup reduced-fat sour cream
1/4 cup reduced-fat mayonnaise
3 tablespoons red wine vinegar
1/4 teaspoon salt
1/4 teaspoon freshly ground black pepper
1 1/2 cups shredded smoked trout (approximately 7 ounces)
1/2 cup chopped green onions
2 tablespoons finely chopped fresh parsley
2 tablespoons finely chopped fresh chives
2 teaspoons finely chopped fresh tarragon
Tarragon sprigs (optional)

1. Place potatoes in a medium saucepan; cover with water. Bring to a boil. Reduce heat; simmer 10 minutes or until tender. Drain; cool.

2. Combine sour cream, mayonnaise, red wine vinegar, salt, and freshly ground black pepper in a large bowl, stirring well with a whisk. Add potatoes, smoked trout, and next 4 ingredients (through chopped fresh tarragon); toss gently to coat. Garnish with tarragon sprigs, if desired. Yield: 9 servings (serving size: about ½ cup).

CALORIES 130; **FAT** 5.3g (sat 1.8g, mono 1.3g, poly 0.6g); **PROTEIN** 10g; **CARB** 10.4g; **FIBER** 1.2g; **CHOL** 30mg; **IRON** 1.1mg; **SODIUM** 242mg; **CALC** 50mg

CHIVES

Available year-round, chives have a very mild onion flavor. Both the hollow stems and the flowers can be eaten.

SUPERFAST

SMOKED TROUT, WATERCRESS, AND ORANGE SALAD

Peppery watercress and sweet oranges play beautifully off the rich flavor of smoked trout. Use arugula in place of half or all the watercress, if you like.

1/2 cup vertically sliced red onion
1 teaspoon grated orange rind
1/3 cup fresh orange juice (about 2 oranges)
1 tablespoon extra-virgin olive oil
1/8 teaspoon salt
6 cups trimmed watercress (about 3 ounces)
1 1/2 cups smoked trout (approximately 7 ounces)
1 cup orange sections (about 2 oranges)

1. Combine first 5 ingredients in a large bowl.

2. Add watercress and remaining ingredients; toss gently to coat. Yield: 6 servings (serving size: about 1 cup).

CALORIES 136; **FAT** 6.4g (sat 1g, mono 3.7g, poly 1.3g); **PROTEIN** 13.4g; **CARB** 6.1g; **FIBER** 1g; **CHOL** 35mg; **IRON** 1mg; **SODIUM** 204mg; **CALC** 57mg

SUPERFAST

SPANISH-STYLE TUNA AND POTATO SALAD

With some of the same ingredients as a salade niçoise, this filling salad features smoked paprika for a richer flavor.

1 pound small red potatoes, quartered
1 pound haricots verts, trimmed and cut into 2-inch pieces
2 cups cherry tomatoes, halved
1/4 cup thinly sliced shallots
3/4 teaspoon salt
1/2 teaspoon smoked paprika
1/4 teaspoon ground red pepper
1 (5-ounce) can albacore tuna in water, drained
1/4 cup extra-virgin olive oil
3 tablespoons sherry vinegar
5 cups torn romaine lettuce

1. Place potatoes in a large saucepan; cover with water to 2 inches above potatoes. Bring to a boil; cook potatoes 6 minutes or until almost tender. Add beans; cook 4 minutes or until beans are crisp-tender and potatoes are tender. Drain; rinse with cold water. Drain.
2. Place potato mixture in a large bowl. Add tomatoes and next 5 ingredients (through tuna); toss. Drizzle oil and vinegar over potato mixture; toss to coat. Arrange 1 cup lettuce on each of 5 plates; divide potato mixture evenly among plates. Yield: 5 servings.

CALORIES 239; **FAT** 11.7g (sat 1.6g, mono 7.9g, poly 1.3g); **PROTEIN** 10.3g; **CARB** 25.6g; **FIBER** 6.7g; **CHOL** 10mg; **IRON** 2mg; **SODIUM** 470mg; **CALC** 81mg

SMOKED PAPRIKA

Pimentón, *or smoked paprika, is a signature flavor component of Spanish cooking and comes in three varieties:* dulce *(sweet),* agridulce *(bittersweet), or* picante *(hot). Deeper red and coarser than Hungarian paprika,* pimentón *colors stews and soups, and is the most widely used spice in the Spanish kitchen.*

SUPERFAST

TUNA AND WHITE BEAN SALAD

For a sustainable seafood choice, buy solid white (albacore) tuna. Look on the label for pole-caught fish.

20 asparagus spears
1 tablespoon capers, rinsed and drained
1 tablespoon chopped fresh flat-leaf parsley
2 tablespoons white wine vinegar
2 tablespoons fresh lemon juice
2 tablespoons extra-virgin olive oil
1 tablespoon butter, melted
1/4 teaspoon salt
1/4 teaspoon freshly ground black pepper
1 cup cherry tomatoes, quartered
1 (15-ounce) can organic white beans, rinsed and drained
4 cups torn butter lettuce (about 1 head)
2 (5-ounce) cans solid white tuna packed in olive oil, drained and broken into chunks

1. Snap off tough ends of asparagus spears. Steam asparagus, covered, 3 minutes. Drain and rinse with cold water; drain.

2. Combine capers and next 7 ingredients (through pepper) in a small bowl, stirring well with a whisk.

3. Place ¼ cup vinaigrette, cherry tomatoes, and beans in a small bowl; toss gently to combine.

4. Place 1 cup lettuce on each of 4 plates, and top each serving with 5 asparagus spears. Spoon about ½ cup white bean mixture over each serving, and divide tuna evenly among servings. Drizzle each salad with about 1 tablespoon vinaigrette. Yield: 4 servings.

CALORIES 270; **FAT** 14.6g (sat 3.5g, mono 7.4g, poly 2.5g); **PROTEIN** 20.2g; **CARB** 16g; **FIBER** 5.6g; **CHOL** 24mg; **IRON** 2.4mg; **SODIUM** 467mg; **CALC** 65mg

SUPERFAST

TUNA, ARUGULA, AND EGG SALAD WITH PITA CHIPS

If your budget allows, try a premium jarred tuna like Ortiz, which is rich, firm, and meaty. And purchase precooked, peeled eggs from your supermarket.

3 tablespoons fresh lemon juice
2 tablespoons extra-virgin olive oil
1 teaspoon Dijon mustard
1/4 teaspoon freshly ground black pepper
1/8 teaspoon salt
6 cups loosely packed baby arugula
1 cup cherry tomatoes, halved
1/2 cup very thinly vertically sliced red onion
1/4 cup kalamata olives, halved
1 tablespoon capers, rinsed and drained
2 hard-cooked large eggs, halved
1 (5-ounce) can light tuna packed in olive oil, drained
2 ounces plain pita chips

1. Combine first 5 ingredients, stirring with a whisk. Drizzle dressing over arugula; toss gently to coat. Divide arugula evenly among 4 bowls; top evenly with tomatoes and next 5 ingredients (through tuna). Serve with pita chips. Yield: 4 servings (serving size: about 2 cups salad and ½ ounce pita chips).

CALORIES 269; **FAT** 17.1g (sat 2.7g, mono 10g, poly 3.2g); **PROTEIN** 13.7g; **CARB** 16.2g; **FIBER** 2.5g; **CHOL** 115mg; **IRON** 1.3mg; **SODIUM** 635mg; **CALC** 78mg

CAPERS

Capers have a pungent, briny flavor and make a nice addition to salads, vegetables, seafood, and chicken dishes. They're the flower buds of a bush native to the Mediterranean. Capers come either packed in brine or salted. Be sure to rinse them to remove extra salt before you use them.

MAKE-AHEAD

TUNA-FENNEL PASTA SALAD

Sure, premium oil-packed tuna is a splurge, but the texture and rich flavor are worth it.

8 ounces uncooked penne (tube-shaped pasta)
1 (7.8-ounce) jar solid white tuna packed in oil
1 lemon
1 Fuji apple, thinly sliced (about 1½ cups)
1 small fennel bulb with stalks
½ teaspoon salt

1. Cook pasta according to package directions, omitting salt and fat. Drain pasta in a large colander over a bowl, reserving ½ cup cooking liquid. Rinse pasta under cold water; drain.
2. Drain tuna, reserving 2 tablespoons oil. Grate 2 teaspoons rind from lemon; squeeze 3 tablespoons juice. Combine reserved oil, rind, and juice in a large bowl; stir with a whisk. Add pasta to oil mixture, tossing to coat. Fold in tuna and apple.
3. Remove fronds from fennel bulb; finely chop fronds to measure 3 tablespoons. Remove and discard stalks. Thinly slice fennel bulb. Stir fronds and sliced fennel into pasta mixture. Add reserved pasta liquid and salt, tossing to coat pasta salad evenly. Yield: 4 servings (serving size: 2 cups).

CALORIES 411; **FAT** 12.1g (sat 1.9g, mono 6.7g, poly 2.4g); **PROTEIN** 23.3g; **CARB** 53.3g; **FIBER** 5.1g; **CHOL** 17mg; **IRON** 2.8mg; **SODIUM** 549mg; **CALC** 52mg

TUNA

The most consumed finfish in the United States, tuna are endangered, and as a large fish, they're also likely to be higher in mercury than smaller fish. Choose U.S.-caught Pacific Ocean albacore for the healthiest and most environmentally friendly choice; or substitute U.S.-caught Spanish mackerel in recipes.

NUTRITIONAL ANALYSIS

How to Use It and Why

Glance at the end of any *Cooking Light* recipe, and you'll see how committed we are to helping you make the best of today's light cooking. With chefs, registered dietitians, home economists, and a computer system that analyzes every ingredient we use, *Cooking Light* gives you authoritative dietary detail like no other magazine. We go to such lengths so you can see how our recipes fit into your healthful eating plan. If you're trying to lose weight, the calorie and fat figures will probably help most. But if you're keeping a close eye on the sodium, cholesterol, and saturated fat in your diet, we provide those numbers, too. And because many women don't get enough iron or calcium, we can help there, as well. Finally, there's a fiber analysis for those of us who don't get enough roughage.

Here's a helpful guide to put our nutritional analysis numbers into perspective. Remember, one size doesn't fit all, so take your lifestyle, age, and circumstances into consideration when determining your nutrition needs. For example, pregnant or breast-feeding women need more protein, calories, and calcium. And women older than 50 need 1,200mg of calcium daily, 200mg more than the amount recommended for younger women.

In Our Nutritional Analysis, We Use These Abbreviations

sat	saturated fat	**CHOL**	cholesterol
mono	monounsaturated fat	**CALC**	calcium
poly	polyunsaturated fat	**g**	gram
CARB	carbohydrates	**mg**	milligram

DAILY NUTRITION GUIDE

	WOMEN Ages 25 to 50	WOMEN over 50	MEN ages 24 to 50	MEN over 50
CALORIES	2,000	2,000 or less	2,700	2,500
PROTEIN	50g	50g or less	63g	60g
FAT	65g or less	65g or less	88g or less	83g or less
SATURATED FAT	20g or less	20g or less	27g or less	25g or less
CARBOHYDRATES	304g	304g	410g	375g
FIBER	25g to 35g	25g to 35g	25g to 35g	25g to 35g
CHOLESTEROL	300mg or less	300mg or less	300mg or less	300mg or less
IRON	18mg	8mg	8mg	8mg
SODIUM	2,300mg or less	1,500mg or less	2,300mg or less	1,500mg or less
CALCIUM	1,000mg	1,200mg	1,000mg	1,000mg

The nutritional values used in our calculations either come from The Food Processor, Version 8.9 (ESHA Research), or are provided by food manufacturers.

METRIC EQUIVALENTS

The information in the following charts is provided to help cooks outside the United States successfully use the recipes in this book. All equivalents are approximate.

Cooking/Oven Temperatures

	Fahrenheit	Celsius	Gas Mark
Freeze Water	32° F	0° C	
Room Temp.	68° F	20° C	
Boil Water	212° F	100° C	
Bake	325° F	160° C	3
	350° F	180° C	4
	375° F	190° C	5
	400° F	200° C	6
	425° F	220° C	7
	450° F	230° C	8
Broil			Grill

Liquid Ingredients by Volume

¼ tsp	=					1 ml		
½ tsp	=					2 ml		
1 tsp	=					5 ml		
3 tsp	=	1 tbl	=	½ fl oz	=	15 ml		
2 tbls	=	⅛ cup	=	1 fl oz	=	30 ml		
4 tbls	=	¼ cup	=	2 fl oz	=	60 ml		
5⅓ tbls	=	⅓ cup	=	3 fl oz	=	80 ml		
8 tbls	=	½ cup	=	4 fl oz	=	120 ml		
10⅔ tbls	=	⅔ cup	=	5 fl oz	=	160 ml		
12 tbls	=	¾ cup	=	6 fl oz	=	180 ml		
16 tbls	=	1 cup	=	8 fl oz	=	240 ml		
1 pt	=	2 cups	=	16 fl oz	=	480 ml		
1 qt	=	4 cups	=	32 fl oz	=	960 ml		
				33 fl oz	=	1000 ml	=	1 l

Dry Ingredients by Weight

(To convert ounces to grams, multiply the number of ounces by 30.)

1 oz	=	1⁄16 lb	=	30 g
4 oz	=	¼ lb	=	120 g
8 oz	=	½ lb	=	240 g
12 oz	=	¾ lb	=	360 g
16 oz	=	1 lb	=	480 g

Length

(To convert inches to centimeters, multiply the number of inches by 2.5.)

1 in	=					2.5 cm		
6 in	=	½ ft			=	15 cm		
12 in	=	1 ft			=	30 cm		
36 in	=	3 ft	=	1 yd	=	90 cm		
40 in	=					100 cm	=	1 m

Equivalents for Different Types of Ingredients

STANDARD CUP	FINE POWDER (ex. flour)	GRAIN (ex. rice)	GRANULAR (ex. sugar)	LIQUID SOLIDS (ex. butter)	LIQUID (ex. milk)
1	140 g	150 g	190 g	200 g	240 ml
¾	105 g	113 g	143 g	150 g	180 ml
⅔	93 g	100 g	125 g	133 g	160 ml
½	70 g	75 g	95 g	100 g	120 ml
⅓	47 g	50 g	63 g	67 g	80 ml
¼	35 g	38 g	48 g	50 g	60 ml
⅛	18 g	19 g	24 g	25 g	30 ml

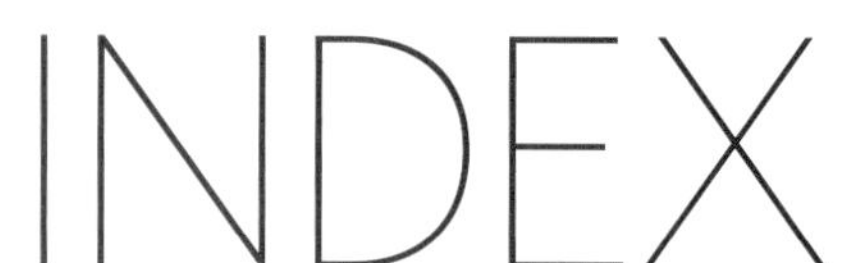

INDEX

A

B

C

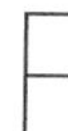

M

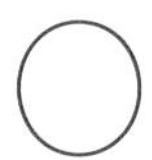

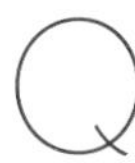

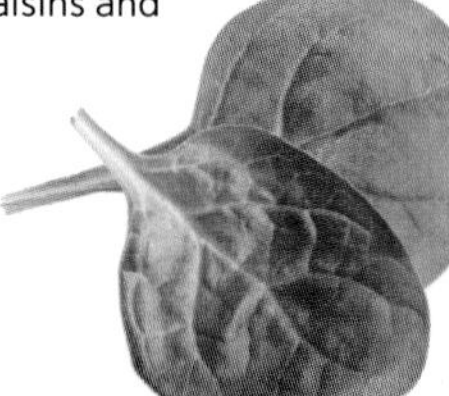